P9-CLO-269

Travellers

MADEIRA

BY
CHRISTOPHER CATLING

Produced by
Thomas Cook Publishing

Written by Christopher Catling
Updated by Frances J. Folsom
Original photography by Jon Wyand
Original design by Laburnum Technologies Pvt Ltd

Editing and page layout by Cambridge Publishing
Management Ltd, Unit 2, Burr Elm Court,
Caldecote CB3 7NU
Series Editor: Karen Beaulah

Published by Thomas Cook Publishing
A division of Thomas Cook Tour Operations Ltd

PO Box 227, The Thomas Cook Business Park,
Units 15–16, Coningsby Road,
Peterborough PE3 8SB, United Kingdom
E-mail: books@thomascook.com
www.thomascookpublishing.com
Tel: +44 (0) 1733 416477

ISBN-13: 978-1-84157-542-1
ISBN-10: 1-84157-542-9

Text © 2006 Thomas Cook Publishing
Maps © 2006 Thomas Cook Publishing
First edition © 2003 Thomas Cook Publishing
Second edition © 2006 Thomas Cook Publishing

Head of Thomas Cook Publishing: Chris Young
Project Editor: Linda Bass
Production/DTP Editor: Steven Collins

All rights reserved. No part of this publication may be reproduced, stored in a retrieval system
or transmitted, in any form or by any means, electronic, mechanical, recording or otherwise,
in any part of the world, without prior permission of the publisher. Requests for permission
should be addressed to Thomas Cook Publishing, PO Box 227, The Thomas Cook Business
Park, Units 15–16, Coningsby Road, Peterborough PE3 8SB, United Kingdom.

Although every care has been taken in compiling this publication, and the contents are
believed to be correct at the time of printing, Thomas Cook Tour Operations Ltd cannot
accept any responsibility for errors or omissions, however caused, or for changes in details
given in the guidebook, or for the consequences of any reliance on the information provided.

The opinions and assessments expressed in this book do not necessarily represent those of
Thomas Cook Tour Operations Ltd.

Printed and bound in Spain by: Grafo Industrias Gráficas, Basauri.

Cover design by: Liz Lyons Design, Oxford.
Front cover credits: Left © Westend61/Alamy; centre © Imagebroker/Alamy;
right © Fotoworld/Image Bank
Back cover credits: Left © Thomas Cook Tour Operations Ltd; right © Thomas Cook Tour
Operations Ltd

Contents

KEY TO MAPS

✈ Airport

★★ Start of walk/drive

1320m ▲ Mountain

[i] Information

☀ Viewpoint

101-3 Road number

Introduction

'I should think the situation of Madeira the most enviable on the whole earth. It ensures almost every European comfort together with almost every tropical luxury.'
H N Coleridge
Six Months in the West Indies, in 1825

The island's abundant blooms are skilfully turned into beautiful bouquets

Madeira is a fascinating blend of contrasting and unlikely ingredients, a place that reminds you of other far-flung destinations, while remaining uniquely itself.

The steep terraced hillsides with their burgeoning banana crops may put you in mind of Bali or the Philippines: English roses and perennials grow in profusion alongside Asian orchids and Indian tulip trees; the island's fragrant eucalyptus woods recall Australia, while the gorse-covered moorlands of the central plateau could be in the Scottish Highlands.

The architecture of Madeira's capital evokes yet another place and time – the

Madeira

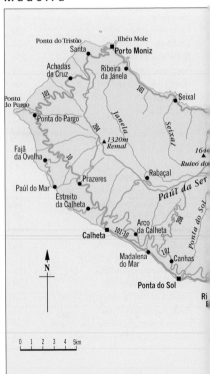

elegant balconies and shaded patios of Funchal seem straight out of the half-real, half-imaginary world of an Isabel Allende or Gabriel García Márquez novel, while its streets depict paving patterns with a more modern aesthetic. On top of all this, Madeira encompasses spectacular ravines and waterfalls, ever-changing skies and seas, and mountain tops where you can enjoy a rare sense of stillness and peace as you admire the magnificent panoramas.

Exploring these lofty and silent peaks it is easy to forget that bustling Funchal is just two hours' drive away. Funchal is also part of Madeira's rich texture and it is a pleasure to return to the capital at the end of a long day's tour, knowing that you can look forward to all the modern comforts of a luxurious hotel and the prospect of an excellent dinner – with or without a glass or two of Madeira.

Nature's profusion is all the more enjoyable when accompanied by such civilised comforts, and that is why Madeira – blessed with both – is such a delightful and satisfying holiday destination.

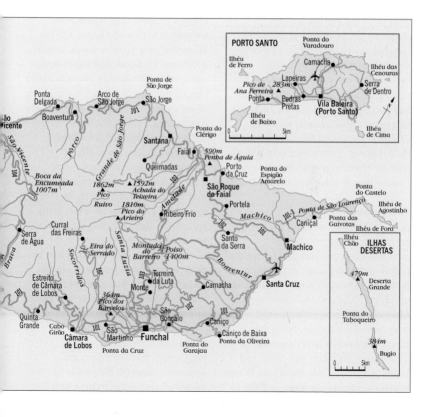

The Land

Madeira is a tiny island set in the Atlantic Ocean, a long way from anywhere. The nearest mainland is the coast of Morocco, 608km away. It is even further to Portugal, the country to which Madeira belongs, for the capital, Lisbon, is nearly 1,000km to the northeast.

Every inch of available land is farmed

Yet Madeira is not entirely alone: it is partnered by the smaller island of Porto Santo, 37km to the northeast, a popular summertime destination for Madeirans because of its long beach and golden sands. Another group of islands, the Ilhas Desertas, lies 16km to the southeast and is usually visible from Funchal; the islands live up to their name (Deserted Isles) by being uninhabited except for birds, seals and visiting naturalists. Much more distant, and also uninhabited, are the **Ilhas Selvagens** (Wild Islands) which lie 216km to the south; they also belong to the Madeiran archipelago, even though they are closer to the Spanish-owned Canary Islands than they are to Madeira.

The Terrain

Madeira is about the same size as Singapore, but beyond that all comparisons cease. You could drive the length of flat Singapore in under an hour, but the same journey would take up to half a day on mountainous Madeira. Distances are magnified by the steepness of the terrain. From the island's main east–west mountain range, numerous high ridges run north and south to the coast. All roads have to take a tortuous zigzagging route in order to negotiate the deep valleys and ravines that lie in between. This contorted terrain was very aptly described in a 19th-century guidebook which recounted a meeting between Christopher Columbus and Queen Isabella of Spain. The queen asked Columbus to describe Jamaica to her. He picked up a piece of paper, crumpled it between his hands and put it down again, saying 'This will give you a better idea of the island's appearance than any of my words'. Precisely the same will do for Madeira.

Another antiquated guidebook describes Madeira poetically as 'surrounded by an abysmal ocean'. The truth of this is brought home as you tour the island, especially the northern side where great Atlantic waves break against the high cliffs that line this coast. Sea and land meet abruptly on the island, with no gently shelving beaches in between – just a jumble of jagged rocks and grey pebbles. Below the waterline the cliffs continue for 1,000m or more before reaching the seabed.

Madeira's Economy

Surrounded by such a deep and dangerous element, the people of Madeira have tended to turn their backs upon the sea, and the island's tiny fishing fleets employ only a handful of hardy adventurers. Instead, most Madeirans make their living from the hard graft of agriculture, tending the land by hand because there is no space on the narrow terraces for machinery. Sugar, known as 'white gold', made the early settlers rich until competition from New World plantations drove prices down. Today it is the yellow gold of bananas and the liquid gold of Madeira wine that sustain the island economy, along with tourism and handicrafts, including wickerwork and embroidery.

Madeira also benefits from funds from so-called 'emigrants' – islanders who have gone abroad to seek their fortune working in the Venezuelan oil industry, or in shops, restaurants and hotels in Britain, South Africa or Australia. The money they send home to help their families is a very significant element in the island's invisible economy and it explains why there are so many banks based in Funchal, competing against each other for the emigrants' accounts.

Madeira in Figures

Population: 280,000 (of whom 86 per cent live on the sunny south of the island, including 115,000 in the capital, Funchal).
Area: 738 sq km.
Length: 56km east to west.
Width: 23km north to south.
Highest point: Pico Ruivo (1,862m).
Sea depth: 6,000m in the Canary Basin, which lies 83km to the west of Madeira.

The drama of Madeira's volcanic peaks is enhanced by the play of the elements

The shimmer of a rainbow perfects a picture-postcard landscape

Climate

Madeira is blessed with an almost perfect climate – it is never intolerably hot and never too cold. In winter, the island's southerly latitude and the warmth given off by the sea combine to ensure that temperatures do not often dip below a pleasant 18°C. This makes Madeira a popular destination for anyone seeking an escape from the icy grip of northern European winters.

In summer, the trade winds help to keep Madeira cool, and clouds build up to screen the island from the hot midday sunshine so temperatures rarely exceed 24°C. This makes Madeira a popular destination for mainland Portuguese visitors along with anyone else fleeing the searing heat of continental summers (by contrast, Madeirans themselves,

looking for some really hot sunshine for a change, go and roast themselves on neighbouring Porto Santo, which in summer is usually very hot and dry).

Despite the equable nature of Madeira's climate, there is also great variety: temperatures drop rapidly with altitude, and chill winds can blow on the mountain tops even in summer; that is why the stallholders who sell sweaters on the top of Pico do Arieiro (1,818m) enjoy a brisk trade.

In winter you can often enjoy the experience of playing with snowballs on the mountain peaks in the morning and sunbathing by the hotel pool in the afternoon.

Even more enthralling is to walk among the high peaks of Madeira in brilliant sunshine, while below you cottonwool clouds shroud the island; you will feel on top of the world, especially since you know that less fortunate souls down at sea level are probably sheltering from the rain.

Rain can be guaranteed to freshen up every day – only in July and August is it likely to be dry. Fortunately, in Funchal, the rainfall tends to come in short bursts: after a clear start to the day, clouds build up and there is often a downpour by noon, so that the late afternoon and evening are clear and sunny once again.

Walking is a pleasurable activity throughout the year

History

20 million years ago	Volcanic eruptions under the Atlantic build up layers of lava to create the Madeiran islands.
1.7 million years ago	Madeiran volcanoes become extinct. Volcanic soils nurture the dense woodland that cloaks the island.
2,000 years ago	Though known to Phoenician, Roman and North African sailors the uninhabited islands are never colonised.
1418	One of the many expeditions sponsored by Prince Henry 'The Navigator' (son of King João I of Portugal) is blown off course by violent storms. Captain João Gonçalves Zarco finds shelter off an island which he names Porto Santo (Blessed Port) in gratitude.
1420	Returning to explore further, Zarco discovers what he calls Ilha da Madeira, the Island of Wood.
1425	Settlement begins in earnest. Early settlers grow rich producing 'white gold' – sugar cane.
1452	The first slaves are brought from Africa and the Canaries to build Madeira's terraces, dig the irrigation channels and work the fields.
1478	Christopher Columbus visits Madeira to buy sugar. He later marries Filipa Moniz, daughter of Bartolomeu Perestrello, first governor of Porto Santo.
1514	The first census reports 5,000 inhabitants.
1542	The defensive walls around Funchal built as protection from pirates.
1566	1,000 French pirates attack Funchal, loot the island and kill the governor and 250 Madeirans.
1580	Philip II of Spain occupies Portugal, and Madeira comes under Spanish rule.
1614	Population is 28,345, including 3,000 slaves.
1640	The Portuguese revolt against Spanish rule, and regain their independence under King João IV.

1662	Catherine of Braganza, daughter of King João IV, marries Charles II of England. Granted commercial privileges, English merchants settle on Madeira, increasingly dominating the Madeira wine trade.
1775	Slavery is declared illegal in Portugal.
1803	600 are drowned when flash floods inundate Funchal. The city's three rivers are enclosed by high walls to prevent future disasters.
1807–13	British troops are garrisoned on Madeira to prevent Napoleon invading the island.
1852	In the same year, cholera carries off 7,000 victims, and the island's vineyards are devastated by mildew.
1887	Economy boosted by European tourists visiting for the winter, or staying en route to South America and the Far East.
1916–17	German U-boats twice shell Funchal from the harbour, causing minor damage.
1931	Troops from Lisbon are used to put down a general strike protesting the regime of the Portuguese dictator, Salazar. Madeirans begin emigrating in large numbers in search of a better life.
1949–58	Flying-boat services operate between Southampton and Madeira.
1964	First commercial flights from Santa Catarina.
1974	Portugal enters a new era of democracy.
1976	Madeira becomes an autonomous region, with a regional government and president.
1986	Portugal's entry into the European Community gives Madeira access to development funds.
1997–2000	The island's south-coast expressway transforms life on the island.
2000	João Jardim elected president for the sixth time.
2002	Madeira adopts the euro.

Governance

The winds of political change came late to Madeira. Until 1968, it had to endure the totalitarian regime of the Portuguese dictator, António d'Oliveira Salazar. Salazar's successor, the marginally more liberal prime minister, Caetano, was then deposed in the Carnation Revolution of 1974: the military took control but symbolised their desire for peaceful change by carrying flowers in their gun barrels.

Porto Santo, one of Madeira's small islands

Creating a New Democracy

At the time of the 1974 revolution there were many in Madeira who wanted complete independence from Portugal. This reaction was understandable – during the long years of the Salazar regime, Madeirans were made to feel as if they were helpless inhabitants of a remote little island who would be lost without mother Portugal. At the beginning of every day, Madeiran school children were made to repeat: *A nação é tudo; tudo pela nação* (the nation is all; all to the nation). This fine-sounding slogan was used to disguise an ugly truth: the Lisbon government had been milking the Madeiran economy for decades, appropriating revenues from exports and tourism, so that what should have been a prosperous island was left with some of the worst poverty and deprivation in Europe.

Politically-active Madeirans were determined that islanders should in future be in charge of their own destiny; they were eventually persuaded that it might be better to remain part of Portugal, but as an autonomous region.

This means that Madeira now controls its own economy and sets its own taxes and customs duties as well as deciding how much should be spent on health, welfare and educational programmes. The island still looks to the Portuguese mainland for its foreign and defence policies, and the brightest Madeiran students still go to Portugal for their university education, but since 1974 there has been a growing sense of island identity; the people of Madeira are proud of their history and culture and now tend to think of themselves as Madeirans first and foremost, rather than as Portuguese.

The System of Government

Madeira, Porto Santo and the other islands of the archipelago make up what Madeiran newspapers call the RAM (Região Autónoma da Madeira). This is governed by the 50-seat regional parliament, based in Funchal, which has the power to pass legislation and deal with all issues directly affecting the islands. In practice, many of the day-to-day decisions are taken by the executive committee, consisting of the president, the vice-president and six secretaries. The island also has a number of town councils responsible for more local issues and, on a broader stage, Madeira elects five representatives from the regional parliament who sit as members of the Lisbon-based Portuguese parliament.

Parties and Personalities

Madeira's head of state since 1976 has been Dr Alberto João Jardim, an extremely popular and charismatic figure whose picture appears almost daily on the front page of Madeiran newspapers as he cuts the ribbon to inaugurate a new school or health clinic. President Jardim's PSD (Popular Social Democrat) party holds most of the seats in the regional parliament and regularly polls 70 per cent of the vote in elections, which are held every four years.

Dissent, such as it is, centres around the PS (Socialist) party and the right-of-centre CDS. The smaller parties are better represented at town council level, and it is here that a conflict of policies occasionally takes place. It is hard, though, for opposition parties to dent President Jardim's popularity because he has presided over decades of unprecedented growth, during which the living standard of most Madeirans has improved very substantially. Today, most villages have electricity, schools, a health clinic, as well as a road link to the capital, Funchal, all of which were just a politician's dream in the 1970s.

Madeirans overwhelmingly re-elected Jardim and the PSD in 1996, and again in 2000, and there is no requirement for him to retire. Rapid economic changes during his tenures have successfully diverted attention from earlier issues of under-development to those concerned with the consequences of rapid growth, including pollution, uncontrolled building and abandonment of the land resulting from Madeira's greater prosperity.

Government offices in Funchal

Tales of Discovery

Many stories have been told about the discovery and colonisation of Madeira, and many myths persist to this day. One is that Madeira is the last vestige of the drowned continent of Atlantis; another is that the lost treasure of the notorious pirate, Captain Kidd, is buried on one of the Ilhas Selvagens.

The truth is more prosaic. It is known for a fact that the Madeiran islands were familiar to navigators long before Porto Santo and Madeira were officially 'discovered' by João Gonçalves Zarco in the year 1420.

Pliny, the 1st-century AD Roman writer, called them the 'Purple Islands' because of the distinctive colour of Madeira's volcanic rocks and soil. The Medici map of 1351, drawn by Genoese cartographers, was the first to depict Madeira and give it a name – Isola delle Lolegname (Island of Wood). The same name – Ilha da Madeira in Portuguese – was used by Zarco when he landed in 1420, laying claim to the island on behalf of Portugal.

The Story of Robert Machin

Facts, though, are rarely as romantic as the tales embroidered by sailors with time on their hands as they sailed the Atlantic carrying cargoes of Madeiran sugar, grain and wine. About 100 years after Zarco's discovery, chronicler Valentine Fernandes published a different account, which he no doubt heard in some harbourside bar. This concerns a Bristol merchant, Robert Machin, who was blown out into the Atlantic by a storm while sailing to Portugal. Ending up within sight of Madeira, Machin went ashore to investigate. His mutinous crew decided to

Christopher Columbus is reputed to have lived in Madeira

abandon Machin, but they got caught up in another storm which drove them on to the Moroccan coast where they were taken prisoner, destined to serve as galley slaves.

Determined to return to civilisation, Machin built himself a raft. He, too, fell prey to Moroccan pirates and ended up in the same prison as his former crew. Machin then furiously attacked one of his fellow sailors, meaning to kill him in revenge. Astonished by the ferocity of the fight, Machin's gaolers forced him to explain his actions and it was not long before the whole story of the mysterious island at the edge of the known world began to circulate. It was only a matter of time before Henry the Navigator heard the story and sent Zarco out to investigate.

Even more romantic versions of Machin's story circulated in the 17th century in which he is portrayed as an English aristocrat eloping with his sweetheart, Anna d'Arfet (or Anne of Hertford).

Shipwrecked on Madeira, she dies of exposure and he of a broken heart. Zarco is said to have found their graves when he stepped ashore in 1420, inspiring him to name the spot Machico. Another Madeiran legend has it that Zarco set fire to Madeira – this being the fastest way to clear the island's dense woodland – and that the forests blazed for seven years.

In fact, clearance was probably much more selective: the island's timber was a valuable resource, used for building houses, ships and the crates in which sugar and other crops were packed.

Columbus and Madeira

Another colourful and persistent story has it that Christopher Columbus lived on both Madeira and Porto Santo for several years; here he married, fathered his only son, and became convinced by the exotic plant remains washed up on Madeira's shores that sailing westward would bring him to the spice islands of the Indies. He therefore sailed back to Lisbon determined to raise funds for an expedition to test his theory.

The story sounds too neat, too well honed to be true, and for many years the Madeirans themselves were among the most sceptical.

Nowadays, however, it looks as if the legend may contain some truth, and that Columbus may have even returned to live on Madeira, off and on, after his discovery of the New World.

For the 1992 quincentenary celebrations, Madeirans decided to acknowledge and capitalise on the Columbus connection for the first time, and visitors to Porto Santo (pp140–2) can now visit the Casa de Colombo (House of Columbus) museum, with its portraits of the great man and early maps of Madeira and the Americas.

Culture

Madeira is an island in transition from third-world levels of poverty to first-world prosperity. The change, not yet complete, has nevertheless been so rapid that you can simultaneously glimpse scenes from Madeira's past and from its future as you tour the island.

Shouldering a bundle of firewood: traditional Madeiran life is arduous

Driving into the village of Santana, for example, you are quite likely to catch sight of what looks like a walking haystack – a peasant farmer invisible beneath the great stack of hay that she is carrying to feed her cow. She and her family may well live in a traditional thatched A-framed house and cook in the open air over a wood fire. She may wash herself and her clothes in a nearby *levada* (irrigation canal), and the family may survive on an income of around €200 a year. Her husband will work tiny terraced fields by hand and will think nothing of carrying the produce he grows in wicker baskets – for very long distances along steep and winding mountain paths – to be left by the roadside for the local co-operative to collect.

Roads and Change

Until recently there were still villages and farms on the island that were two hours' arduous walk from the nearest road, which had no electricity or television and where some of the inhabitants had never travelled to see the island's capital, Funchal.

The number of Madeirans who live this traditional life – spending all their waking hours in laborious work without the benefit of modern technology – has dwindled rapidly in recent years. Road-building programmes, partly funded by European Union grants, have been a major catalyst for change. As new roads have been driven further into the remotest parts of Madeira's interior, electricity has followed, generated by wind turbines located on the island's northern cliffs, or by water turbines powered by the outflow from reservoirs. Roads mean that farmers can drive their crops to the agricultural co-operative or sell direct to hotels and restaurants. Many now travel to Funchal every Friday to sell their produce in the lively Mercado dos Lavradores (Workers' Market).

As villages have been linked into the island's road network, the land-hungry have arrived: urbanites looking for plots on which to build a weekend home and emigrants returning from overseas with a nest egg looking for somewhere to build a retirement home. To the despair of those who love the island's traditional architecture and natural beauty, many scenic villages are now almost surrounded by newly-built villas, and the green hillsides splattered with bright orange roof tiles and white walls. To complete the transformation, tourists can now reach almost every corner of the island by coach or taxi, and shops, restaurants and even hotels have been opened to cater for them. Many villages have benefited from a general increase in prosperity.

Town and Country

It is difficult to predict what long-term effect these changes will have on the culture of Madeira, although Funchal offers some clues as to how the rest of the island may develop. The Catholic church, which is still a major force in the lives of rural Madeirans, has far less power in the capital – so much so that many parish churches in Funchal are locked and unused. Where religious processions to honour the Virgin or a patron saint draw crowds of devotees in the village, only events such as the New Year festivities and the Madeira Wine Rally attract similar numbers in the city. Funchal people see themselves as sophisticated and cosmopolitan, intellectual and, where religion is concerned, at best agnostic. Yet loyalty to the family remains as strong as ever it was and the people of Funchal are every bit as hardworking and entrepreneurial as their country cousins. What is more, there is a strong sense of pride in the things that make Madeira special and unique – its wines, landscapes and architecture, and even the traditional costumes and dances, which are worn and performed for pleasure and not merely to earn tourist revenue.

A wall plaque illustrates a scene now rarely witnessed – carrying produce to market the old way

Festivals

If one goes by the pervasive air of celebration, almost every day seems to be a festival day on Madeira. But festivals are still announced in the traditional way, by setting off a string of explosive firecrackers and shooting rockets into the air. In the days before telephone, post or newspapers, this was an effective way of inviting your neighbours to come across and join in the fun.

The Virgin is honoured throughout Madeira at Assumption (15 August)

Most village festivals (called *arraiais*) are rooted in the Catholic religion and are held to honour the local patron saint or to celebrate a major event in the church calendar – the **Feast of the Assumption** (15 August) is one of the biggest, and local celebrations often begin a full fortnight in advance of the day itself. The day will begin with Mass, and processions of children and villagers dressed in their best singing hymns. The parish priest, or perhaps the bishop of Funchal, will preach a long sermon about the perils of drinking and dissipation, but by nightfall everyone (including the priest) will be dancing and singing beneath trees illuminated with coloured bulbs, the band on the makeshift stage alternating between Madeiran folk songs and the latest pop chart hits. For visitors, such festivals offer the chance of sampling local wine and *espetada* kebabs cooked the way they should be, over the embers of a vinewood fire.

Other festivals and events are more formal and, with one eye to tourism, have been elaborated in recent years to increase their appeal to visitors. Here is a list of the main events to look out for:

February
Carnival is celebrated in villages all over the island, but the costumed parades held in Funchal are the best. The parade, held on the Saturday before Shrove Tuesday, features satirical floats poking mild fun at the authorities, accompanied by bands and fireworks, while a second parade on Shrove Tuesday itself features clowns and fancy dress.

April/May
Madeira's **Flower Festival**, held on a weekend at the end of April or early in May, sees Funchal transformed into a blaze of colour. Streets, houses, shop windows and churches are decorated with ribbons, flags, floral carpets and pictures made of flowers. The climax is a parade of flower-smothered floats through the city's main streets.

May/June
Madeira's **Music Festival**, at the end of May and beginning of June, is a chance to hear students of the local *conservatoire* perform, as well as guest musicians from around the world. Most of the concerts are held in the cathedral and the elegant Teatro Municipal.

August

Car fanatics regard the **Madeira Wine Rally** as one of the toughest stages of the European championships and celebrities from all over Europe pour in for the event. If you are in Funchal for the start of the rally in early August you will hear the ear-ripping sound of the rally-car engines. The best way to follow the action is by watching it on TV.

Madeira's biggest religious festival takes place on 15 August, when devout Catholics from all over the island visit Our Lady's church at Monte (*see p88*), climbing the steps to the church on their knees, to honour the Assumption of the Virgin Mary.

September

Wine festivals in Funchal and Câmara de Lobos feature wine tasting, dancing in the streets and demonstrations of grape treading (*see pp76–7*).

December

Christmas preparations begin as early as 8 December when *bolo do mel* (honey cake) is traditionally made and when children plant wheat, maize or barley seeds in small pots. About ten days later the pots begin to sprout a head of fresh green shoots, symbolising renewal and plenty in the year ahead. The pots are placed round the crib figures, which are found not just in churches but also in shop windows, village squares, hotel foyers, restaurants and private homes. From 8 December, Funchal's streets are lit up nightly with coloured bulbs and illuminations, in preparation for the island's spectacular **New Year's Eve** festival (*see pp20–1*).

Carnival features some truly spectacular and ingeniously designed costumes

New Year

New Year on Madeira is the climax of the island's festive calendar. From 8 December, the city of Funchal will have been ablaze every night, with nearly half a million coloured bulbs outlining the shapes of buildings, draped over trees, and illuminating the waterfront promenade. As New Year approaches, Madeiran emigrants from South America, Australia, Canada and southern Africa fly home to be with their families, joining the hundreds of tourists who jet in to enjoy the warmth of a Madeiran Christmas, and the many sea voyagers – in small boats and in huge luxury liners – who all set sail for Funchal's harbour.

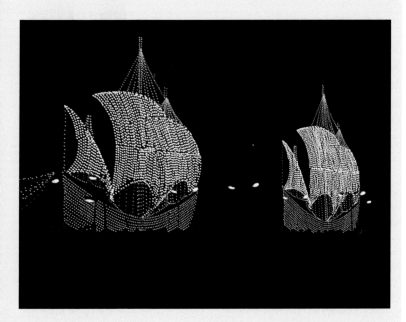

On New Year's Eve itself another migration begins as Madeirans from all over the island head for Funchal in cars, trucks and buses, clogging all the approach roads. The aim of all this movement is to be in Funchal for one of the world's most spectacular fireworks displays. As midnight approaches on New Year's Eve, the lights are turned on in every building in Funchal and its suburbs, doors are opened and curtains drawn so that the whole amphitheatre of hills enclosing the city seems a blaze of lights, matched by the lights of the ships and boats in the harbour. Silence falls, and then, as the bewitching hour strikes, all Funchal explodes with the sound of ships' sirens, the popping of champagne corks, church bells ringing, and the cheers of onlookers, all accompanied by a meteor storm of coloured rockets bursting overhead. Those who have seen it once regularly return, which is why hotel rates double over the Christmas and New Year period – if you want to be there yourself, be certain to book at least a year in advance.

Champagne corks and fireworks all reach for the sky at midnight on New Year as brightly-lit ships host parties in the harbour

Impressions

When Zarco first caught sight of Madeira in 1420 it was covered in cloud and he thought he was approaching the edge of the world – the place where, according to medieval cosmography, demons and evil spirits dwelled. By the time Zarco landed he had changed his view entirely and rapturously described the island as a place of 'lightsome beauty… the land of fairies'.

Trees hide Funchal's main promenade, the Avenida do Mar, from the sea

Today's traveller, arriving by air, still experiences a sense of journeying across endless ocean until the jewel-like island, intensely green and set in a crystal clear blue sea, suddenly appears on the horizon. All too quickly that vision is lost as you descend to Santa Catarina airport and are whisked off, with great efficiency, through the Funchal traffic to your hotel.

Once you have settled into the hotel, it is easy to be seduced into spending all week by the poolside, strolling through the streets of Funchal, or lingering for hours over lunch in some harbourside seafood restaurant. It is easy to forget that glimpse you had of the green mountains rising out of the sea – all too easy, in fact, to become part of that statistic that says 80 per cent of Madeira's visitors do not travel beyond the confines of Funchal. That would be a pity because the island's coastal and mountain landscapes are some of the most spectacular in Europe, moreover they are also very accessible, by coach tour or taxi.

Planning your Time

The best strategy for enjoying the real Madeira is to spend the first day or so unwinding and getting to know Funchal; then take a tour on the second or third day of your stay.

Too many people leave seeing the island until the last moment, signing up for a round-the-island tour towards the end of their visit, only to discover what pleasures they have missed all week. Nor does it make sense to try and see all of Madeira in a day: a typical island tour covers 150km, most of the day spent in a coach, yet covering only a fraction of the island's varied charms.

It is far better to split Madeira into two, and visit the western and eastern sides separately. Most tour operators operate the two separate tours on different days, which allows you to see the two contrasting sides of Madeira by coach, minibus or covered jeeps.

If you are travelling with a tour operator, remember that while their excursions are a bit more expensive than those offered on the street, the extra few euro guarantee you only one language on the coach.

Remember, too, that the skies are often clearer in the morning than the afternoon, and while there is always risk of cloud, mist or rain during the day, the views may be far better if you take a pre-lunch rather than post-lunch tour.

Travelling Independently

Many tour operators will also organise taxi excursions for you, which is actually preferable to negotiating directly with the taxi drivers themselves.

A good tour operator will be able to find you a reliable taxi driver who will drive carefully (it is easy enough to suffer from travel sickness or vertigo on Madeira's steep and winding roads), who knows the island thoroughly, and who speaks English (or any other language) fluently.

Taxis can usually be hired by the half-day (9am–1pm or 1–5pm) or the full day; though the rates are supposed to be fixed by the taxi drivers' association, most drivers try and charge somewhat more, so you should be ready to bargain them down.

If only two people are sharing a taxi, then the cost will be slightly higher than if they take a coach tour, but if three or more people are sharing the price of the taxi, then the taxi fare works out cheaper.

The first view on arrival: Madeira's Santa Catarina airport

Official taxis in Funchal's main square

Touts

Madeira is remarkably free, so far at least, of timeshare touts and similar nuisances, but they do exist, and it is best to be forewarned. Timeshare touts are paid large sums of money to get you to sign an irrevocable and expensive contract, and they will use every tactic possible to get you to do so. These touts tend to hang around the Hotel Zone, so if you are pestered by them, return to your hotel at once.

Considering the high numbers of repeat clients with a high disposable income, timeshare has taken off in a large way over the last few years, with most of the newest five-star hotels selling up to 30 per cent of their rooms on a 30-year timeshare basis.

Instead of dealing with touts, it is better to contact reputable companies – for instance, Porto Bay, owner of three hotels on the island, and Pestana, the largest hotel owner in Portugal. These two companies have new flagship properties, for both normal hotel bookings and timeshare ownership.

Avoid unlicensed drivers offering tours or taxi services; some of them are also timeshare touts, and besides, they charge exorbitant rates.

The yellow licensed taxis operate with fixed or metered fares (*see pp183–4*). Most taxi drivers are honest, but be wary of seeking their advice, especially on which restaurants are best. They will offer to take you somewhere good, cheap and typically Madeiran: and all too often that restaurant will be located so far out of town, that you have to pay a higher taxi fare, and it will be at such a distance from any other restaurant that you will have no choice but to eat there. By the time you discover it is also twice as expensive as downtown restaurants, the driver will have disappeared (he will be back later to collect his commission from the restaurant owner).

If you are aware of these tricks, they are easy to avoid, and you should have a carefree, enjoyable holiday.

Thomas Cook's Madeira
The first reference to a Cook's holiday to Madeira is in 1885, when the island was included as part of a trip to the Portuguese mainland. In the early 20th century, steamers, which resembled 'floating hotels', departed regularly from London and Liverpool to make round-trip cruises to Madeira, calling at the Canary Islands as well. In the *Traveller's Gazette*, in 1921, Madeira was described as 'this flower-bedecked isle under Ionian skies'.

A hair-raising ride on the Monte toboggan

Funchal

Madeira's capital is an elegant city, once dubbed 'little Lisbon' by visiting mariners because of the grandeur of its cathedral and harbourside buildings. The city resembles a huge amphitheatre sheltered by a semicircle of hills, with open views out across the harbour to the sea and the distant Ilhas Desertas.

The hills rise steeply above Funchal

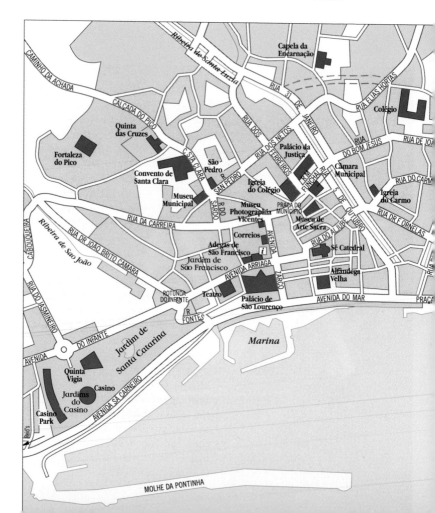

Most of Madeira's hotels occupy elevated positions to the west of Funchal, built on the cliff tops and hills to make the most of the views. From this Hotel Zone it takes up to 30 minutes to reach central Funchal on foot, or a few minutes by taxi. Madeirans themselves complain about traffic and pollution in the capital, and the diesel fumes can be oppressive during the morning and evening rush hours (around 9am and 5pm), but visitors from many other cities will consider Funchal delightfully quiet.

Central Funchal

Measures have already been taken to route traffic out of the elegant avenues at the very heart of the city. One of these is Avenida Arriaga, lined with trees, gardens, fountains, fashionable shops, and belle époque mansions, now the prestigious premises of banks and government departments (see Central Funchal walk, pp60–1).

Traffic still uses the Avenida do Mar, the city's wide seafront promenade, but this is an ideal spot from which to admire the short but colourful Madeiran sunset, or for taking an after-dinner stroll (see To the Waterfront walk, pp58–9). To the right of the avenue is the busy harbour area filled with container ships and cruise liners.

This deep natural harbour helped Funchal edge out Machico, which rivalled Funchal in size and prosperity, to become the island capital. The great **Molhe da Pontinha**, the breakwater which surrounds the harbour, was built in 1895 and incorporates the tiny fortified island of **Loo Rock**, midway down its long concrete arm.

More fortifications survive to the landward side of Avenida do Mar, including the Palácio de São Lourenço. Bristling with cannons, it was built in the 1520s to defend the city against repeated piratical attacks, and later converted into the residence of the island's 19th-century governors, one civil and one military.

Following Avenida do Mar to its easternmost limit you will reach the Zona Velha, or Old Town (*see* The Old Town walk, *pp62–3*), with its narrow cobbled alleys and outdoor restaurants serving some of the best-value food to be had in the capital. Between the Hotel Zone and the Zona Velha lives the rest of the city (*see* Between the Rivers and Elegant Mansions walks, *pp64–5 & pp66–7*), a wonderful jumble of modern and old, where stylish shops aimed at cruise passengers sit side by side with antiquated general stores selling daily necessities and smelling of salt cod and dried herbs.

The architecture is equally varied, and further colour is added by the many flowersellers and street traders who operate around the cathedral and **Mercado dos Lavradores** (or Workers' Market), itself a fascinating amalgam of sights and sounds.

In short, Funchal may be a small city, but it is not to be underestimated – each time you think you have covered every inch of the ground you will turn a corner and discover something entirely new.

City of Fennel

The name Funchal comes from *funcho*, meaning fennel. Zarco gave this name to the spot where he landed in July 1420 because of the abundance of the sweet-smelling herb that he found in flower.

Funchal's deep natural harbour, with the Hotel Zone beyond

It pays to look down wherever you walk in Funchal, to admire the style and craftsmanship of the humble pavements. In the Zona Velha, the streets are made from sea pebbles – rounded by the waves, carefully selected so that they are all of the same size – which are set in mortar. The cobbles are hardwearing and quickly drain the water away when it rains.

Funchal's main square, the Praça do Município, is elegantly covered in a repeated series of fan shapes, alternately laid in dove-grey basalt and white marble. More flamboyant is Avenida Arriaga, with its heraldic flowers and *fleurs-de-lis* in black and white mosaic. In some parts of the city the paving is now sadly patched with asphalt where service trenches have been dug, but the art of making mosaic pavements is not dead: recently completed examples include the large Madeiran coat of arms in

Praça de Cristovão Colombo, south of the cathedral, and the caravel, compass, sedan chair and wine-carrier with his yoke in Rua João Tavira, northwest of the cathedral.

Decorated paving on Avenida Arriaga (above), Funchal; and (below) the Praça do Município

Storage in oak barrels helps to impart flavour to Madeira wine

Adegas de São Francisco

A visit to the Adegas de São Francisco (the St Francis Wine Lodge) is one of the most enjoyable ways to spend a couple of hours on Madeira, and if you are planning to take home a bottle or two of Madeira it is worth coming here first to learn about the history and production of this magnificent fortified wine.

The wine lodge is run by the Madeira Wine Company, a consortium whose shareholders include most of the famous names of the Madeira trade: Blandy, Leacock and Luiz Gomes. Everything about the lodge has the appropriate patina of time, and as soon as you enter you will be greeted by the delicious smell of old wood and wine. The timber

buildings surround a cobbled courtyard overlooked by a wisteria-clad balcony. Some of the buildings date back to the 16th century and were part of the island's Franciscan friary which closed in 1834 following the dissolution of all monastic orders operating in Portugal.

Standing in various rooms around the lodge are huge barrels of mahogany and American oak; some 400,000 litres of precious wine are stored in this lodge alone, but this is a small fraction of the 1 million litres a year produced by the Madeira Wine Company alone and of the 4.5 million litres produced by the seven wine companies operating in the island.

The sheer weight of these storage barrels means that the floors of the wine lodge have to be very strong – hence the massive timbers used as joists and supports are said to have come from ships either wrecked on Madeira or dismantled for salvage once they were no longer seaworthy.

Guided Tours

If you join one of the excellent hour-long guided tours offered by the wine lodge you will first be shown an audio-visual presentation detailing the history of Madeira wine. Next you will visit the coopers' yard to watch wine barrels made of oak being repaired, cleaned or marked with branding irons. You will then be taken to the warming rooms where the wine is heated in vast vats for six months using the natural warmth of the sun, assisted by hot-water pipes. Heating is essential to the character of Madeira wine, though its effects were discovered quite accidentally.

The original Madeira, known as *malmsey*, was a pretty ordinary wine which sailors drank because it was cheap. Barrels of *malmsey* served the double duty of providing ballast and alcoholic stimulation on long sea journeys. Sailors then discovered that the wine improved when it was taken to the tropics, spending weeks or months in a hot hold. Now the wine does not leave Madeira until it has been bottled, but until the end of the 19th century it was still sent on board ship to the equator and back as an essential part of the production process. The other key ingredient is brandy, added to stop the fermentation and fortify the wine, after which the slow process of maturation begins.

As the tour reaches its conclusion you will be taken round a small museum full of leather-bound ledgers, ancient wine presses and old tools, before returning to the downstairs wine bar for a free tasting. After a glass or two of delicious wine you may be tempted to make a purchase, but don't get carried away – some of the rare bottles on offer cost over €250!

Avenida Arriaga 28. Tel: (291) 223065. Open: Mon–Fri 9am–1pm & 2.30–6pm, Sat 9am–1pm. Guided tours: Mon–Fri at 10.30am & 3.30pm, Sat 11am. Admission charge for the guided tours.

Museum piece: an ancient wooden wine press

Madeira Wine

BLANDY'S
MADEIRA

There are four basic types of Madeira, each named after the variety of grape from which they are principally made. *Sercial* is an amber-coloured dry wine, often served as an aperitif or with soup or fish. It is made from grapes grown at around 800m; grapes grown at lower levels increase in sweetness because more of their sugars are concentrated by the sun. Thus, *verdelho*, grown at around 500m, is a medium dry, tawny-coloured wine taken with the main course. The nutty rich *bual* goes well with Stilton or chocolate, while the sweetest Madeira is the rich, dark, mellow *malmsey*, good with after-dinner coffee.

The gradual heating and cooling of the wine and the fortification with cane spirit (a type of brandy) gives Madeira its extraordinary longevity. A reserve wine will already be 5 to 20 years old and vintage Madeira must have spent 20 years in the cask and two in the bottle, but these are relative youngsters.

The oldest surviving bottle dates to 1772 – when the cork was last replaced in 1991 the wine inside was analysed and found to be perfect. You can find wines for sale on Madeira at around €300 that were bottled in 1863, while the American Civil War was still in progress.

Winston Churchill, a regular visitor to Madeira, was fond of the island's noble wines and pointed out that history was being sipped with every glass. At a dinner held at Reid's Hotel in 1950, the British community in Madeira presented Churchill with a bottle that had

previously been given to Napoleon when he anchored off the island on the way to exile in St Helena, but the full bottle was never drunk and came back to Madeira. Opening it and sharing it with his fellow guests, Churchill was not so much impressed by the Napoleon connection as by the thought that 'this wine was made when Marie Antoinette was still alive!'

History is imbibed when you sip Madeira, taking in aromas that – in some cases – have taken many decades to mature

Alfândega Velha

The Alfândega Velha (Old Customs House) is one of Madeira's most ancient buildings, begun around 1477. In the 1970s it was converted to form the home of Madeira's regional parliament. For this reason it is open to the public only on rare occasions (if it is open, do go in to see the fine wood-carved ceiling) but you can walk around the exterior to look at the Manueline-style decoration of the stone-carved portals.

The harbourside façade is now hidden by the modern circular debating chamber clad in white marble and widely held to be a blot on the face of a dignified building.
Rua da Alfândega. Not normally open.

Convento de Santa Clara

The Convent of the Order of Poor Clares was founded in the 15th century by two grand-daughters of the island's discoverer, João Gonçalves Zarco. Zarco himself, having lived to the ripe old age of 80, was buried beneath the high altar of the conventual church. His simple tomb slab is not visible, and an imposing 15th-century tomb at the rear of this church is often mistaken for Zarco's; in reality it belongs to his son-in-law, Martin Mendes Vasconcelos.

Much of the rest of the church was rebuilt in the 17th century and the walls are lined from floor to ceiling with a carpet-like tapestry of yellow, white and blue *azulejos* tiles, making a rich geometric pattern. The timbered ceiling features a painted ship in full sail, as well as floral and heraldic motifs.

The heavy iron grille at the back of the church has an interesting story.

Behind it is a stout wooden door which would be opened so that visitors could have limited communication with the nuns who lived in the convent beyond.

It is a reminder of the very isolated and withdrawn lives led by nuns who could not leave their cloistered confinement – though the nuns of this convent did once flee their home in 1566, to escape a piratical attack, journeying inland to the hidden valley now named Curral das Freiras (Nuns' Refuge) in their honour (*see pp84–5*).

The Tragic Story of Maria Clementina

Many of the nuns were condemned to a life within convent walls by pious or penurious parents, and the case of one such nun became a *cause célèbre* in the 19th century: many foreign visitors to Funchal went to the convent to visit her, providing what little companionship and comfort was possible talking through a metal grille.

Maria Clementina was widely held to be the most beautiful girl on Madeira but her parents forced her to take the veil on her 18th birthday because they were unable to afford the dowry, without which aristocratic young ladies found it hard to find a husband of similar rank. (Placing your daughter in a nunnery was also supposed to confer spiritual benefits on parents and child alike.)

A year later, the newly established liberal government in Lisbon ordered the religious houses of Portugal to liberate any of their inmates who had been forced into taking monastic vows and who wished to leave.

Maria was released, and fell passionately in love with a handsome army officer. Before they could marry, however, Portugal's absolutist monarch dissolved the parliament and revoked all its laws. Maria was forced to return to the convent where she spent the rest of her life.

Abuses such as this eventually led the Portuguese parliament to dissolve all religious establishments, though today the Poor Clares have returned to Santa Clara, where they run a highly-regarded school, part of which you will see if you wander through the convent to find the lovely, peaceful 15th-century cloister, planted with citrus trees, which lies to the south of the church.

Calçada de Santa Clara. Open: daily 10am–noon & 3–5pm, except during church services.

If the church door is closed, ring the bell at the convent entrance to the right of the church, for admission.

Santa Clara's tranquil convent cloister, built soon after the island's discovery

Madeira had no indigenous population when Zarco landed in 1420, but the island soon attracted adventurers of all nations – Flemish, Italian, Spanish, French and English. Many came as merchants who invested in land and made fortunes from sugar cultivation and the wine trade. English involvement in the island increased substantially after Charles II married Catherine of Braganza, daughter of King João IV of Portugal, in 1662. England very nearly gained Madeira as part of Catherine's dowry; it is said that the

scribe who drew up the marriage contract was Madeiran and that patriotism led him to omit the island. English traders moved in anyway when Charles II passed a law in 1665 prohibiting the export of European goods to the English colonies in America, unless they were shipped through English ports in English ships. Madeira was explicity excluded from this restriction, and one result was the rapid growth of wine shipments from the island to the colonies. The Americans grew to like Madeira wine so much that it was used to toast the signing of the Declaration of Independence in 1776. The lucrative trade also helped establish some of the island's oldest merchant families, such as the Blandys and the Leacocks, who are still very much in business today.

Foreign tourists have also had a major impact on the island, whether coming for the good of their health, or escaping from the cold northern European winter, or stopping en route to India, the Far East, South Africa or South America. Only the wealthy could afford to come to Madeira, hence the genteel up-market image which still prevails today, though this is now being rapidly eroded by an explosion of mass-market tourism, following the extension of the airport runway in 1985 and the large-scale development of the Hotel and Tourist zones of Funchal.

Facing page: To many visitors calling at Madeira on a luxury cruise, taking the Monte toboggan ride is still the ultimate thrill
Above: Sightseeing olden style by hammock

The English Church and British Cemetery

Madeira's English church is a circular, domed building in Neo-Classical style which opened in 1822. The architect was Madeira's British Consul, Henry Veitch, who had to work within the constraints of Catholic Portuguese law. This reluctantly allowed the Protestant community on Madeira to build a place of worship, so long as it did not look like a church. The galleried interior is light and airy, lit by fan-shaped windows around the base of the dome, and brightened by fine flower arrangements. Surrounding the church is a well-tended garden containing a bust of Philippa of Lancaster, daughter of John of Gaunt and mother of Prince Henry the Navigator, whose marriage to King João I of Portugal in 1387 established the long-standing Portuguese–English alliance. Attached to the nearby chaplaincy is a library containing some 2,500 volumes in English.

The British Cemetery is a short walk away, a beautiful and poignant spot full of flowers, lizards, birds and butterflies. Opened in 1887, it contains moving memorials to Protestants of all nations, not just the British. Many record the short lives of hopeful visitors who came to Madeira in search of relief from consumptive diseases but did not long survive. You can also read memorials to several of the German, Polish, Danish and American physicians who came here to treat them.

The English Church, Rua do Quebra Costas 18. Open: 9am–5.30pm. Services: see p183.
The British Cemetery, Rua da Carreira 235. Open: daylight hours (ring the bell at the gate for entry).

IBTAM Handicrafts Institute

Crafts are such an important part of the Madeiran economy that this institute was set up to provide training and monitor standards. It is principally concerned with the arts of embroidery, tapestry and wickerwork. A small museum on the first floor of the institute's headquarters building displays some very fine examples of all three.

Climbing the stairs to the museum you will be greeted by a massive tapestry *The Allegory of Madeira*, designed by Gino Ramoli and made between 1958 and 1961. The tapestry depicting a typically flower-filled Madeiran landscape, contains a total of 7 million stitches, the work of 14 girls.

The museum itself consists of cases full of embroidered tablecloths, bedspreads and diaphanous nightgowns, all of which will appeal to the connoisseur of fine needlework.

Also on display are some interesting examples of island costume, including colourful hand-embroidered waistcoats, blouses and scarves, and a small exhibition showing how embroidery designs are transferred, using inked rollers, to the fabric before the embroiderers begin their work.

Rua do Visconde de Anadia 44. Open: Mon–Fri 10am–12.30pm & 2.30–5.30pm.

Igreja do Colégio

The Baroque façade of this collegiate church dominates Funchal's main square, though it is not the most attractive on Madeira, and the gesticulating Jesuit saints filling the niches look in danger of toppling over in their frenzy of religious ecstasy.

The interior is more likeable, with its geometric *azulejos* tiles and its altar surrounds, carved in gilded wood and plaster, featuring fat pink cherubs climbing through a tangle of vine leaves. The decoration mostly dates from the period 1641 to 1660 though the church itself was founded in 1574, soon after the Jesuits were granted permission to establish a college, or seminary, on Madeira.

After the Jesuits were expelled from Portugal in 1759, the college was turned into a military barracks. It has now been designated part of the campus of Madeira's embryonic university.
Praça do Município. Open: daily 5–6pm & for services.

Colourful contrasts: the façade of the Jesuit church fronting Funchal's main square

Jardim Botânico

The whole of Madeira is one vast botanical garden where plants grow in extraordinary profusion, thanks to the combination of fertile volcanic soils, sunshine, regular rainfall and high humidity. If you are interested in plants, the Botanical Garden is the place to learn more about the island's exotic flora. Even if you are not a plant buff, you will enjoy the magnificent setting and the views.

Visitors to the gardens leave their mark

Natural History Museum

The Botanical Garden first opened to the public in 1960. Before that it was a private estate appropriately called the Quinta do Bom Successo (Good Fortune Estate) belonging to the Reid family, founders of Reid's Hotel (*see pp170–1*).

The Reids' former residence now houses a Natural History Museum located just inside the entrance gates. This contains cases full of fossils, fish, insects and stuffed birds – all of which look rather dusty with age and far from lifelike. There are, however, one or two more impressive exhibits, such as the massive piece of fossilised tree heather (*Erica scoparia*) which would have grown to an even greater girth had its life not been ended by volcanic eruptions 10 million years ago.

The Garden

Immediately around the museum is an area devoted to orchids (in flower from November to March). Another area is planted with species indigenous to Madeira – plants which are not found anywhere else in the world in the wild. Some of these have, of course, been disseminated by botanists and horticulturalists to other parts of the world since their original discovery, including the *Geranium maderense* (Madeiran cranesbill) with its handsome ferny foliage and masses of magenta flowers.

Paths radiate from the museum to various points of the garden. If you want to explore the site systematically, climb to the top of the garden first, to the so-called Lovers' Grotto and viewpoint. Once this *miradouro* overlooked a deep green ravine; now the foreground is filled with the sight of a new expressway, which might cause the gardens to lose their role as a tranquil refuge from city life.

From this high point, a series of terraces descends down the hillside to an open-air café, set amid carp-filled ponds, and rampant stands of papyrus grass. The lower terraces are more regimented than the woodland areas higher up – indeed, one area is devoted to commercial plants grown for the cut-flower trade and as seasonal bedding.

The bedding plants are planted in geometric patterns designed to show off their foliage colours, ranging from sulphur yellow to grey and deep purple; one block even spells out *Benvindo* (welcome) in beetroot red.

After this the sparse simplicity of the cactus and succulent beds comes as something of a relief to the eye. If you are lucky, some of these splendid and massive plants will be in flower, the exotic colours of the blossoms contrasting with the sculptural simplicity of the trunk and branches.

Even if there are no blossoms, the dense and intricate cobwebs threaded between the prickly leaves provide an opportunity to study closely the island's varied spider population.

Caminho do Meio, Quinta do Bom Sucesso (3km from Funchal).
Gardens open: daily 8am–6pm.
Museum open: daily 9am–12.30pm & 1.30–5.30pm.
Admission charge.
Bus: 29, 30, 31 from Funchal or taxi.

Geometrical virtuosity executed in colourful foliage

The African Tulip Tree, or Flame of the Forest, blooms in the Jardim dos Loiros

Jardim dos Loiros

While exploring the Jardim Botânico (*see pp40–1*) you will hear a constant chorus of hoots, whoops and screeches emanating from the adjacent property. If your curiosity is aroused you can try to discover the source of all this noise by taking a short downhill walk from the entrance to the Botanical Garden to the Jardim dos Loiros (Tropical Bird Garden). Here, amid well-tended gardens, are the noise-makers: some birds flying freely where they want, and others within the aviaries dotting the grounds. The various cockatoos, parrots and parakeets are as gaudily coloured as the flowers and some reveal even more striking colours when they open their wings to fly. You will enjoy the sight of

these colourful birds so long as your conscience is not troubled by the knowledge that they are kept in such an unstimulating environment. A bare concrete cage is a long way from the South American jungle.
Caminho do Meio. Open: daily 9am–6pm. Admission charge. Bus: 29, 30, 31 or taxi from Funchal.

Jardim Orquídea

This tiny garden, located some 200m from the Jardim Botânico (*see pp40–41*) allows you to view the different processes involved in commercial orchid production. During the flowering season (from the end of November to early April), the shade houses and polythene tunnels are full of exotic blooms – some spidery, some fat and waxy, spotted or plain, and in every colour from brown, black and purple to electric blue, yellow and green.

For the rest of the year, the garden is not one of Madeira's most compelling attractions unless you are an orchid fanatic because there is little to see except for displays covering the propagation and development of orchid seeds.
Rua Pita da Silva 37. Open: daily 9am–6pm. Admission charge. Bus: 29, 30, 31 or taxi from Funchal.

Jardim de Santa Catarina

If you walk to central Funchal from the Hotel Zone on a regular basis you will soon get to know this public park on the hillside overlooking the harbour. A mini botanical garden, it contains a number of fine specimen trees planted in the late 1940s when the garden was converted from a disused cemetery. Fountains and aviaries dot the park, as do some industrial relics – a steamroller and a sugar-cane mill, for example.

There is also an open-air café and a children's adventure playground. A bronze sculpture of a sower, the work of Francisco Franco (*see p48*), stands on the main lawn of the park, while lower down, near the Capela de Santa Catarina, is a statue of Christopher Columbus and a modernistic fountain featuring a prone female torso.

The chapel itself dates from 1425, built on the orders of Zarco's wife, Constança Rodriguez, and is the oldest place of worship on Madeira.

The body of the little chapel has been rebuilt several times – most recently in the 17th century – but the porch still shelters the original holy water stoup,

carved with the wheel of St Catherine. *Avenida do Infante. Open: 24 hours.*

Jardim de São Francisco

This most central of Funchal's public gardens offers a shady retreat close to the Tourist Information Centre and is a popular place where Madeirans, young and old, meet to gossip and pass the time of day. It also contains some magnificent trees (most of which are labelled) planted in the 19th century, when Franciscan monks, along with all religious orders, were expelled from Portugal.

This garden was created for public use on the site of their ruined convent, and amid the lush foliage you can still see the stone-carved coat of arms which once decorated the convent gateway. *Avenida Arriaga. Open: 24 hours.*

Symbol of Madeira's fertility, Francisco Franco's statue of the *Semeador*, the Sower

Mercado dos Lavradores

The Workers' Market is one of the most compelling and colourful sights on Madeira, a bustling place which touches on all aspects of island life, not just food. Friday is the best day to visit it because peasant farmers from all over the island arrive in the market on that day, bringing their produce for sale. Makeshift stalls are set up in the streets and in the car park to the south of Rua de Carlos I.

Even if you do not want to shop, the market is worth visiting for the magnificent displays, especially those of the costumed flower sellers at the entrance to the covered market, and those of the fruit and vegetable vendors on the ground floor. Those who are squeamish about seeing fish being gutted and filleted should, perhaps, give the basement fish market a miss.

The prices, both for fruit and for fish, are extraordinarily low, and you will soon realise why most of the island's farmers have to survive on a very meagre income. Even so, most market traders usually find a few euros to spare when the lottery ticket sellers do their rounds of the market, offering the chance to win that dream ticket to end all financial worries.

Rua Dr Fernão Ornelas. Open: Mon–Fri 7am–8pm, Sat 7am–2pm, closed Sun.

Museu de Arte Sacra

This museum will delight the art connoisseur in you. Housed in an 18th-century building that was once the Episcopal Court, is a priceless collection of Renaissance Flemish paintings, considered to be the best in Portugal.

In the 15th and 16th centuries Portugal's trade with Flanders was very strong, creating a market for Flemish art. Government and church officials, along with plantation owners were anxious to decorate their churches and residences with these spiritual works of art.

Opened in 1955 the museum was created specifically for these paintings, many of which had been left neglected for years in residences and churches all over the island. An ambitious restoration programme by the Museu de Art Antiga in Lisbon, the country's foremost restoration museum, was started in the 1930s to save these master paintings from virtual rack and ruin.

The Flemish collection, displayed on the top floor, has the works such as *Descending from the Cross*, by Gerard David (1460–1523), *The Annunciation* by Joos Van Cleve (1508–45) and the *Triptych of Santiago Menor and Sao Filipe* by Pieter Coecke Van Aelst. Also on display is a very moving 16th-century oak sculpture of Christ from the Flemish school and Marinus Van Reymers' portrait of St Jeronimo.

The middle floor of the museum has displays of clerical garments, delicately embroidered vestments and church silver. Definitely not as interesting as the Flemish art, but worth a look.

Rua do Bispo 21. Open: Tue–Sat 10am–12.30pm & 2.30–6pm, Sun 10am–1pm. Admission charged.

Produce to tempt all the senses on sale in the bustling Workers' Market

The flower sellers of Funchal's Mercado dos Lavradores (*see p44*) all wear the distinctive costume of the island. For women this means a striped woollen skirt worn with a red embroidered waistcoat, beautiful pleated blouse, and a shoulder scarf. Red is the dominant colour, but the scarlet stripes of the skirt alternate with yellow, black, green, blue or white stripes – the precise colour combinations differ from one village to another, as do

the embroidery patterns on the scarf and waistcoat. Similarly, the colours in the waist sash worn by the men provide a clue to their home village. The sash is worn with a white linen shirt and baggy, knee-length trousers. You will often see men wearing bobble hats as you tour the island, knitted with ear-flaps as a precaution against the cold winds that can blow above 800m. For special occasions both men and women wear

the *carapuça*, a small black or blue skull cap with a long tassel. Both sexes also wear boots called *botacha*. These are made of naturally tanned cowhide and goatskin, with the upper part turned down to the ankles and trimmed with a red band. Madeiran song and folk dance groups, who regularly perform in Funchal's hotels and restaurants, take their art very seriously and aim to keep island customs alive – they will show you and explain different parts of their costume. There is a small display of authentic historical costume, showing regional variations, in the IBTAM museum (see p38).

Facing page above: Wind protection for the ears; below: Folk dancers in traditional costumes
Right: Madeiran costume is as bright as the island's flowers; below: Soft, supple boots enable Madeirans to walk long distances

Museu Cidade do Acucar (Sugar Museum)

Formerly housed in the Town Hall, this museum, located north of the beautiful Praça de Colombo, has been reduced drastically in its exhibits documenting Madeira's sugar trade. The museum now occupies the building that was the home of João Esmeraldo, a 14th-century sugar merchant.

Locally the house is known as 'Columbus's House' because reportedly Christopher Columbus was a guest of the Esmeraldo family in 1498.

The original house was demolished in 1876. During excavation in 1986 several important archeological finds were revealed including the house's original well, given a place of honor in the museum. Sadly, most of the exhibits and the timeline of Madeira's history that decorated the walls of the Town Hall are not in the new museum. What is on display are a few sugar moulds dating to the 15th century and some 16th century, ceramics and religious icons.

The museum is not something to go out of your way for; stop in if you are at the Praça de Colombo.
Praça de Colombo.
Open: Mon–Fri 10am–12.30pm & 2–5pm. Free admission.

Museu Fortaleza

The Fortress Museum is located within the bastions of the Palácio de São Lourenço entered through a splendid 16th-century carved stone portal. The museum traces the history of the fortress from its construction in the 1520s to its later conversion into the official residence of the island's two governors – one military, one civilian. On display are historic guns, cannon, armour and photographs of the palace as it is today, complete with titillating 19th-century ceiling frescoes of Neptune and a retinue of blowzy mermaids.

Photographs are as close as you can get to the main building, which is still the residence of Madeira's armed forces' Commander-in-Chief and guarded by goose-stepping, sword-carrying soldiers. *Avenida Arriaga (opposite the tourist information office). Open: Free tours on Wed at 9.30am & Fri at 3pm, but you will need to schedule a tour by calling (291) 202530 or visit the main tourist office. The National Palace can be visited only if you have had a previous appointment with the office of the Prime Minister. Free admission.*

Museu Franco

Art lovers should make the effort to see this excellent but quiet museum displaying the work of the two Franco de Sousa brothers. Henrique (1883–1961) was a painter and Francisco (1855–1955) was a sculptor. Though born on Madeira, both spent much of their lives working in Lisbon and in Paris, where they were much influenced by the artistic milieu of Picasso, Degas and Modigliani.

Henrique experimented with various styles, so there are numerous displayed canvases here that will remind you of Van Gogh, Gauguin and Cézanne, but he eventually found his forte as a portrait painter; his pictures are fresh, colourful and airy, and he endows all his sitters with character and nobility, be they peasants with fascinating, weatherworn faces or pampered aristocrats seated in their gardens.

Francisco is the better known of the two brothers simply because his statues, such as the Zarco monument marking the centre of Funchal and the *Semeador* (Sower) in the Jardim de Santa Catarina, are familiar city landmarks. The displays covering his work include a number of commemorative statues, working drawings, lithographs, as well as his designs for medals, coins and postage stamps.

Rua do João de Deus 13.
Open: daily 10am–12.30pm & 2–6pm.
Free admission.

Cannon muzzles protrude over the poinsettia-clad walks of the São Lourenço fortress

Museu Frederico de Freitas

This absorbing museum is in two parts. The first consists of hundreds of cartoons, engravings and paintings of Madeira, most of them dating from the 19th century, hung round the walls of a two-storey gallery. The eyes glaze over after a while faced with such a mass of material, much of which derives from the hand of amateur artists.

Even so, it is interesting to see how these artists have responded to the island's dramatic landscapes, so different in their elemental force from the gentle pastoral scenes that the artists were trained to draw. There is also an amusing sequence of pictures by Isabella de França from the journal she kept on her visit to Portugal and Madeira in 1853–4. Isabella was honest enough to admit her paintings were a bit crude, but they do record what she experienced with frankness and humour.

All these pictures were bequeathed to Madeira in 1978 by the lawyer Dr Frederico de Freitas, along with his house, which forms the second part of the museum. This charming old residence was built in the late 17th century by the Counts of Calçada, but with splendid Art Nouveau additions, including the little *salon vitré* (conservatory) in the garden designed for sitting in and admiring the views, and the wonderful, intimate Winter Garden, with its cane furniture, doors and hanging lamp, all in the Art Nouveau style. The stately rooms are crammed with objects collected by Dr de Freitas, from fine furniture, carpets and religious paintings to an extraordinary collection of some 2,000 jugs.

There is also an important collection of handpainted *azulejos* tiles but the most endearing items are the crib figures and Madonnas carved in wood in the 17th and 18th centuries, some from the distant outposts of the Portuguese empire, such as Goa and Macao.
Calçada de Santa Clara.
Open: Tue–Sun 10am–12.30pm &
2–6pm. Admission charge.

Museu Municipal

The Municipal Museum is much more fun than the rather bureaucratic name suggests. Downstairs there is an aquarium and also displays of stuffed sharks, as well as birds, mammals and other forms of Madeiran wildlife. Younger children will enjoy staring into the gaping jaws of the sharks and imagining what it might be like to be munched by those perfectly vicious, razor-sharp teeth. There are plenty more ugly-looking specimens to feed your nightmares, including bloated prickly porcupine fish and a giant crab with claws almost a metre long. Some of the displays are very realistic. The island's birds, for instance, are shown as if feeding their young in the nest, surrounded by all the debris and droppings you would expect. The aquarium below is pitch dark except for the large tanks containing typical Madeiran fish and marine vegetation: try spotting the flounders, masters of camouflage; wonder at the beauty of the sea anemones; see how crabs walk under water – balletically on the tips of their claws – watched by brooding surly lobsters and weird beasts such as the scorpion fish. Altogether this museum is a good introduction to the island's wildlife as well as being a good place to pass a rainy hour or so.

Rua da Mouraria 31. Open: Tue–Fri 10am–6pm, Sat–Sun noon–6pm. Admission charge.

The inviting Art Nouveau interior of the Freitas Winter Garden

Museu Quinta das Cruzes

The Quinta das Cruzes (literally 'The Mansion of the Crosses') is an elegant and airy house which gives a taste of the lifestyle once enjoyed by Madeira's most wealthy inhabitants. It is said that Grande Capitaō Zarco, Madeira's discoverer and Funchal's first ruler, had his house on this site, splendidly situated high on a hill above the city.

Religious art of Madeira – a painted clay figure

Now the house is surrounded by suburbs, though the world is kept at bay by the high garden wall and the extensive gardens which have been designated as an 'archaeological park'. This means that 15th- and 16th-century tombstones, coats of arms, architectural mouldings and inscriptions have been placed around the garden where rampant vegetation obscures much of their detail but adds to their romantic charm.

The two most striking exhibits are the huge stone window frames set on the lawn to the left of the museum entrance, carved with little man-eating lions, dancing figures and rope motifs. Some would have you believe that these come from the house in which Christopher Columbus lived on Madeira (*see p15*); in fact they date from 1517 and are a fine example of the ornate Manueline style which flourished under the reign of Manuel I of Portugal (1490–1520). In the rest of the garden you will find frog-filled ponds, dragon trees (*Dracaena draco*) with claw-like aerial roots and bark like the skin of a reptile, and a big display of pot-grown orchids (in flower from late November to early April).

The present house largely dates from the early 19th century when the original 17th-century structure was rebuilt by the Lomelino family, wealthy Genoese wine shippers, who furnished it in the typical style of the period. There are many delicate pieces of furniture in the Regency Trafalgar style, made from the local *vinhático* wood (*Persea indica*), similar in colour to mahogany, as well as pieces by Chippendale and Hepplewhite which the owners of the mansion may have purchased from visiting tourists; it was the practice, in the 19th century, for visitors wintering on the island to bring their own furniture and then sell it off at the end of their stay to pay the rent, as well as the servants' wages and the grocer's bills.

Each room of the mansion has a different theme, which you will discover as you explore. Room 4 contains art from India and China imported by the Portuguese East India Company, notably a watery-blue silk wall-hanging embroidered with butterflies from northern India and a rare Cizhou-ware vase made in China in the 13th century. European art features in Room 5, including a Flemish painting by Jean de Mabuse of the *Three Magi* (1470). A huge 18th-century Aubusson carpet and a tapestry of similar date, featuring dancing peasants, sets the theme for the French style of Room 6. In Room 9, do not miss the big oil painting of Funchal, one of several topographical views set about the house. Room 10 contains 19th-century costumes and jewellery – from full dress uniforms to lace and linen nightclothes. In Room 11, there are tender crib figures of painted clay, made in the 18th and 19th centuries.

Downstairs, in the former kitchens and basements, is a miscellaneous collection, including a series of satirical lithographs poking fun at Madeiran dress and manners, especially those of the clergy, who are portrayed as fat and self-indulgent. Here, too, are finds from the Dutch East India ship, the *Slot ter Hooge*, wrecked off Porto Santo in 1724 and salvaged in 1974.

Finally, there are some fine examples of cupboards made out of recycled packing cases – not today's flimsy affairs, but 17th-century packing cases made of stout hardwoods which, once Madeira's sugar trade died, were taken apart and made into furniture.

Calcada do Pico 1. Museum open: Tue–Sun 10am–12.30pm & 2–6pm. Gardens Tue–Sun 10am–6pm. Admission charged. Bus: 15a from Praça da Autonomia.

Furniture, figures and other objects constitute an eclectic collection

Quinta da Boa Vista

The Quinta da Boa Vista, sometimes
referred to by its old name, the Garton
Greenhouses, is well worth visiting if
you are interested in plants and gardens.
The Quinta specialises in growing
orchids for the cut-flower market,
propagating the microscopic seeds (each
seed head can produce 5 million seeds)
and nurturing them through the critical
first four years of their life until the tiny
plants are ready to be taken out of their
test tubes and exposed to the open air.
Extraordinarily delicate in the early
years, they then become unbelievably
tough – surviving, seemingly, in dust-
dry soil with no visible means of
nutrition. Being epiphytes, they derive
their nourishment from moisture in the
air, and Madeira's humid climate
provides ideal living conditions. Though
most orchids flower only in winter (the
first blooms appear in late November
and the flowering period continues until
early April), the lovingly tended gardens
around the Quinta da Boa Vista make a
visit worthwhile at any time of year. You
can also buy orchids and flowers to take
home (*see* Shopping, *p146*).
Rua Lombo da Boa Vista.
Open: Mon–Sat 9am–5.30pm.

Sé (Cathedral)

Funchal's cathedral was begun in 1485
and completed in 1514. Its construction
marked a major stage in Funchal's
development. Previously it had been a
small frontier town at the edge of the
known world, a place full of
adventurers, slaves and refugees, beyond
the reach of law and religion. Now it was
thought worthy of a cathedral and the

Exotics of the plant world: a carefully nurtured
Quinta da Boa Vista orchid

king of Portugal himself, Manuel I, sent
two master-builders to supervise the
work, along with the gift of a fine
processional cross (now in the Museu de
Arte Sacra, *see p44*).

Naturally, the cathedral was built in
the Manueline style, named after the
king, a late Gothic development noted
for inventive decorations reflecting
nautical themes (anchors, ropes, fish)
and the kind of strange birds, animals
and flowers that Portuguese explorers
were beginning to see in newly
discovered parts of the world.

The playful Manueline details of
Funchal's cathedral are best seen from
the streets to the south of the church,
looking up to the barley-sugar pinnacles
rising from the roof near the tower.
Equally exotic are the designs on the nave
ceiling, though these are difficult to see in
the very dark interior: they are picked out
in white ivory against a background of
carved wood from the native Madeiran
tree, variously known as juniper or
prickly cedar (*Juniperus cedrus*). If the
cathedral doors are open they may allow

in just enough light to let you view the choir stalls, carved out of the same wood and painted blue and gold. The stalls depict saints, apostles and evangelists but in the clothing of the 17th century, when they were carved, and so providing an insight into contemporary (male) fashion. Sadly, even with the doors open you will have to take it on trust that the altar is surrounded by 16th-century Flemish and Portuguese paintings – it really is too dark to see, though you can get an idea of the rich splendour if you come here when the chancel is lit up for a service, or for the occasional classical concerts which take advantage of the cathedral's fine acoustics.

Rua do Aljube. Open: daily during daylight hours. Closed for lunch 12.30–2.30pm. Free admission.

A typical Madeiran carved and gilded altar frame in Funchal cathedral

Madeira is still a very religious island, and large sums of money are spent on maintaining and restoring parish churches. Sadly, for the architectural historian, this means that most have been rebuilt several times since their original foundation and the present structures, with their bland Neo-Baroque façades and interiors, seem to be of no great age. If you dig around, however, you may find features that are older and more interesting. Here are some clues on where to look.

First seek out the font at the back of the church – usually housed in a small room, or baptistery, to the north (left as you enter the church). The font is likely to be the oldest surviving feature, because churches have often been rebuilt but the parish will retain the original 15th-century font as a link with the original community. Some are plain hollowed-out boulders, while others (such as the one in Ribeira Brava: *see p105*) are more ornately carved.

The main altar is likely to be the next oldest feature, and although the statuary may be modern, the ornate Baroque altar surround, often of carved and gilded wood, usually dates to the 17th or 18th century and is full of fascinating little details, such as cherubs and butterflies hidden amid a mass of vine leaves and foliage.

The walls of the church may be covered in *azulejos* tiles of similar date – usually handpainted in soft blues and yellows in complex geometric patterns. Pictorial tiles showing scenes from the life of Christ are likely to be more modern and mass produced.

Ceilings do not get repainted very often because of the difficulty of access; many were last painted in the early part of the last century, if not earlier, and floral patterns are common, usually

incorporating examples of Madeira's abundant wild flora. Every church on Madeira has something of interest if you look hard enough, even if it is not of great age.

A favourite with many visitors is the fishermen's chapel in Câmara de Lobos (*see p79*) whose walls are painted with charmingly naïve pictures of the miracles of St Nicholas, patron saint of seafarers.

Modern mass-produced statuary and *azulejos* tiles are typical of many Madeiran churches Some older work survives, such as the carved and gilded woodwork in Câmara de Lobos and Ribeira Brava's Manueline pulpit and font

Walk: To the Waterfront

If you have just arrived in Madeira, this walk is for you. It is designed to give you a route from the Hotel Zone to central Funchal. (*The route is marked in orange on the map below.*)

At a leisurely pace it will take you between 30 minutes and an hour.

Estrada Monumental, the main road through the Hotel Zone, takes all the traffic leaving Funchal for the west of the island on to the new expressway linking Funchal to Ribeira Brava. Put up with the noise and try and enjoy the views towards Funchal, which are especially good around Reid's Hotel (see pp170–1). From here descend Avenida do Infante.

1 Avenida do Infante

Art Deco villas line your left; on the right is the Savoy Hotel and then the modern Casino Park Hotel. The circular casino in the grounds, shaped like a crown, was designed in the 1970s by Oscar Niemeyer, best known for his work in the Brazilian capital, Brasília. Next on the right is a mansion painted a bougainvillaea pink and protected by an armed guard: this is the **Quinta Vigia**, official residence of Madeira's president. *Cross to the opposite side of the road and look for the Hospício da Princesa entrance.*

To the Waterfront (for the green route see pp66–7)

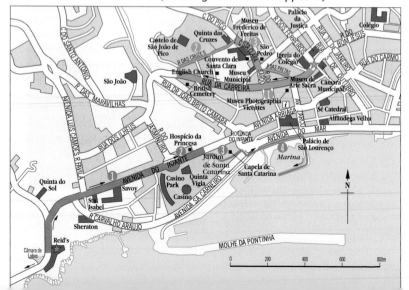

2 Hospício da Princesa

Very few visitors ever find their way into the well-tended gardens of this hospital, though they are open to the public. The hospital itself dates from 1859 when it was founded as a sanatorium for tuberculosis sufferers by Doña Amelia, wife of Emperor Pedro I of Brazil, as a memorial to their daughter, who died from the disease.

Cross the road again to enter the Jardim de Santa Catarina.

3 Jardim de Santa Catarina

This small park will provide you with a good introduction to the botanical richness of Madeira, for it is planted with a good variety of flowering trees and shrubs, some of them labelled. At the centre of the park is the 1919 bronze statue of the *Semeador*, the Sower, scattering seed across the lawns.

To the right of the park there are good views down over the harbour and central Funchal. Paths lead down to the **Capela de Santa Catarina**, said to have been built in 1425 by Constança Rodriguez, wife of Zarco, the island's discoverer. It is, thus, Madeira's oldest church, but the venerable building is always locked and wears an air of neglect.

Looking down from the terrace where the chapel sits, you can see the traffic roundabout known as the Rotunda do Infante. Here is a statue of Henry the Navigator seated beneath a rather ugly stone arch and looking across to a fountain of sea horses supporting a globe (the Central Funchal walk, *see pp60–1*, begins here).

Keep to the right-hand side of the park and a flight of steps will take you down to Avenida do Mar.

4 Avenida do Mar

Those who like boats and marine life will enjoy watching the waterside activities in Funchal's harbour – with luck, a huge ocean-going cruise liner will be in port, or a tall-masted sailing ship. You will also see cargo being unloaded from container ships and boats being repaired. Further along Avenida do Mar is the yacht marina, lined by good seafood restaurants on the landward side. Just before you reach the floating restaurant, turn right and walk out along the sea wall surrounding the marina. This is worth doing for the view as you look back at the island, and for the colourful graffiti painted on the walls by the many people who have sailed to Madeira in yachts from America or Europe.

From here you can join The Old Town walk (see pp62–3), simply by continuing along the waterfront to the Praça da Autonomia.

Sailors' graffiti in the yachting marina

Walk: Central Funchal

Funchal's main avenue, Avenida Arriaga, was laid out at the turn of the 20th century with a wide central carriageway, shaded by trees and equipped with benches, where Madeirans come to stroll and gossip, especially in the evenings. The avenue is lined with noble buildings, shops and art galleries (*see the route marked in green below*).
Allow 2 hours.

Start at the Rotunda do Infante, at the western end of Avenida Arriaga.

1 Rotunda do Infante

The roundabout is named after the Infante, or Prince, Henry the Navigator, who never visited Madeira but sent Zarco to claim the island for Portugal in 1420. The Marina Shopping Centre on

the right is full of upmarket shops and is popular with cruise passengers.
Take the next turning right, Rua do Conselheiro José Silvestre Ribeiro, to the Casa do Turista at the bottom on the left.

2 Casa do Turista

The Casa do Turista, or, as it styles itself, 'The Famous Shop', is more like a

Central Funchal (*for the orange route see pp64–5*)

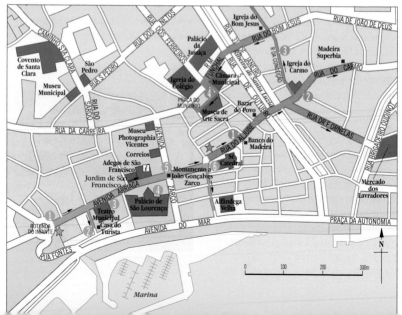

museum than a shop, an elegantly furnished town house where all sorts of tempting displays of embroidery and tableware are laid out beneath ornately plastered ceilings. The shop stocks top-quality crafts not just from Madeira but also from mainland Portugal.

Return up Rua do Conselheiro and turn right to the Teatro Municipal.

3 Teatro Municipal

The Municipal Theatre was built in 1888 and has boxes rising vertically in tiers, modelled on the Little Theatre at Versailles. Often there is an art exhibition in the foyer which enables you to go in and look around. The theatre bar, open to the street with its tree-shaded garden area, is a popular meeting place among Bohemian Madeirans.

Next to the theatre is an even more ornate building, now a Toyota showroom, decorated with *azulejos* tiles showing visitors to the island in the 1920s being carried in a hammock and riding a toboggan from Monte. Opposite is the colourful Jardim de São Francisco (*see p43*), a garden full of tropical trees and shrubs built on the site of the former Franciscan friary, closed in 1834.

4 Palácio de São Lourenço

The next building on the right, with bulky cream-coloured walls, is the St Lawrence Palace, built in the 16th century to defend Funchal from pirate attacks and still the headquarters of Madeira's military command. Sword-bearing soldiers guard the main entrance but there is a small museum open to the public (*see p48*). Opposite are the Tourist Information Centre and the Adegas de São Francisco (or St Francis Wine Lodge), well worth visiting (*see p30*).

5 Monumento a João Gonçalves Zarco

Just beyond the palace, the Zarco monument marks the heart of Funchal. The statue of the island's discoverer was carved by Madeiran sculptor Francisco Franco (*see pp48–9*) and unveiled in 1934. On the northwestern corner of the square is the splendid building of the Banco de Portugal, one of the best in the city, with the decorative details of swags, baskets of fruit and human figures carved in marble and grey basalt contrasting with gleaming white walls.

Across Avenida Zarco is the regional government building with its huge tiled entrance hall and courtyard fountain, while the next building along, the Banco Nacional Ultramarino, has a pretty Art Deco lamp consisting of a bronze maiden symbolising commerce on its entrance stairs.

6 Sé (Cathedral)

Avenida Arriaga ends at the cathedral (*see pp54–5*) on whose north side flower sellers dressed in scarlet embroidered costumes have their stalls (from here you can join the Between the Rivers walk, *pp64–5*). To the south and east lies a warren of little alleys, whose shops are gradually being smartened up to form an attractive pedestrian shopping area.

Two blocks south is the Alfândega Velha (*see p34*), the former Customs House, built in the 16th century and now converted to form the seat of the island's regional parliament.

Walk: The Old Town

Funchal's Zona Velha (Old Town) is a delightful area of the city where the tastes of well-heeled tourists are catered for in restaurants and nightclubs side by side with some of the poorest slums in the city. The area still has a gritty character but is rapidly being developed.

Allow 30 minutes.

Start at the Praça da Autonomia.

1 Praça da Autonomia

In the middle of the roundabout is the Autonomy Monument, celebrating the self-governing status Madeira achieved after the 1974 Carnation Revolution. The monument consists of a woman bursting forcefully out of her imprisonment in a block of bronze. This also marks the point where two of

Funchal's canalised rivers meet and flow into the sea.

To reach the Old Town proper, you can either walk along the sea walls, or follow the café-lined street called Rua de Carlos I which runs parallel, to the north. In between is a plot of land which once served as the bus station, but is now a car park where peasant farmers set up an extension of the Mercado dos Lavradores (Workers' Market) on Fridays.

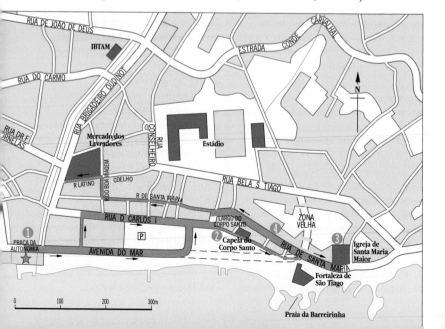

2 Largo do Corpo Santo

This narrow cobbled square gives you a good sense of the Zona Velha's contrasts. Cheek by jowl with numerous pavement cafés specialising in seafood is the shipyard, on the right, belonging to the Madeira Engineering Company, where fishermen's trawlers are repaired. At the far end of the square is the little Capela do Corpo Santo, a simple chapel built by Funchal's fishermen in the 16th century. Beyond the chapel is the Fortaleza de São Tiago, built in 1614 as part of the city's defences. This is now the home of the Museum of Contemporary Art, with works donated by the artists themselves. To the right of the fort, an alley leads through a small shanty town of shacks selling grilled fish to locals who come here to swim from the tiny pebbled beach, the Praia da Barreirinha.

Turn left by the fort up Rampa do Forte, then right to reach the church of Santa Maria Maior.

3 Igreja de Santa Maria Maior

This church is situated in the poorest end of Funchal but has benefited from the opening of the Lido swimming complex. The Lido area has banks, hotels, bars and restaurants. Santa Maria Maior church, opposite the Lido, is also known as the Igreja do Socorro (Church of Salvation) because there is a shrine inside of Apostle St James the Less, who helped end a plague that hit the area in the 16th century. The present church is 18th century and has a theatrical air, with its painted ceiling and glass chandeliers, and its gilded pulpit looking like an opera box.

There are excellent views of the sea and of Funchal from the terrace in front of the church.

Turn right out of the church and follow Rua de Santa Maria all the way downhill.

4 Rua de Santa Maria

This street will take you past Arsenio's Fado Restaurant, a popular night spot where you can hear typical Portuguese *fado* music and song. As you approach the end of the road nearest to the Mercado dos Lavradores, or Workers' Market (*see p44*), you will encounter all the bustle of shoppers, makeshift street stalls and hawkers selling everything from lottery tickets to bunches of garlic and herbs.

Turn right up busy Rua do Boa Viagem and you will soon arrive at the back entrance of the market where fishermen sell their catch. If you would rather not look at the ugly espada fish, turn left in Rua Latino Coelho and walk round to the front entrance where the market teems with people and stallholders selling colourful fruit, flowers and vegetables.

Doorstep conversation in the cobbled pedestrian streets of the Old Town

Walk: Between the Rivers

The first part of this walk is for serious shoppers – there are lots of curious and interesting shops to dip into, muddled up in typically Madeiran style so that shops selling jewellery sit next door to shops selling tap washers or salted cod. The walk then explores the area that lies between two of Funchal's rivers – both canalised as a precaution against autumn rains which can see them rise from a trickle to 4m in depth. *(See the route marked in orange on the Central Fuchal walk map, pp60–1.)*
Allow 30 minutes.

Start in the street that runs northeast of Funchal's cathedral, the Rua do Aljube.

1 Rua do Aljube

There is a good view up this broad street of the cathedral tower with its tile-covered spire, echoed by the tower of the Banco do Madeira, further up. On the left-hand side of the street Teixeiras (No. 15) sells fine embroidered blouses

Igreja do Carmo (Carmelite Church)

in modern styles and Maison Blanche (No. 19) is an upmarket department store. Further up on the right are the stalls of costumed flower sellers under bright umbrellas, and the street widens to form an attractive square. Here you will find the **Bazar do Povo** (Paupers' Bazaar), founded in 1883, a covered shopping mall where numerous retailers on three floors sell everything from table linen and carpets to religious statuary. This lines the whole north side of Rua do Betencourt, which leads to the Ribeira de Santa Luzia. Crossing the river, ponder the fact that 600 people were killed in the floods that hit the city on 9 October 1803. The retaining walls you now see were built between 1804 and 1807 to contain this river and the city's other two rivers as a consequence of that flooding. There have been serious floods several times since, until quite recently.
Cross the river to busy Largo do Phelps. Shoppers may want to explore Rua Dr Fernão Ornelas, to the right, which also

*has interesting shops. Otherwise bear left
to Carmo church.*

2 Igreja do Carmo

If you are lucky you may find the
Carmelite Church open. Inside this
17th-century church, near the high altar,
are two very aristocratic tombs shaped
like coffins resting on the backs of lions,
and *azulejos* tiles depicting scenes from
the life of Christ. If the church is closed,
carry on up Rua do Carmo and you
might have better luck visiting the
embroidery showroom and factory
called Madeira Superbia at No. 27 (first
floor), next to the Cine Jardim and the
Moorish-style building (now a laundry)
at No. 33.

*Retrace your steps up Rua do Carmo and
turn right in Rua da Conceição.*

3 Rua da Conceição

This narrow lane has some of Funchal's
oldest buildings, some in a poor state.
No. 27, for example, is a fine Manueline
building beneath the peeling façade,
17th century in date and well worth
restoring. Already restored are Nos
49–53 with an ornate balcony, central
tower and deep roof eaves. Further up at
No. 71 you may be lucky (if it is a
weekday) to see the blacksmith at work
in his forge. Rua da Conceição continues
the other side of Rua do Bom Jesus; it is
worth continuing up a short way, if only
to see No. 82, on the right, an
embroidery warehouse with tiled façade,
cast-iron balconies and an Art Deco
door made for a giant!

*Back on Rua do Bom Jesus turn right
(east) past the 17th-century Bom Jesus
church and cross the river again. As you*

Mock Moorish in Rua do Carmo

*cross the river look right to see the former
residence of Henry Veitch, who was
British Consul from 1809 to 1836. Veitch
designed the towered house himself and it
is now occupied by the Madeira Wine
Institute.*

4 Praça do Município

On the other side of the river you will
pass the rather ugly Palácio da Justiça
(Law Courts) on the right with a
pollution-stained statue of Justice in
front, and then the more attractive main
square, the Praça do Município. To the
east is the Câmara Municipal, to the
south the Bishop's Palace containing the
Museu de Arte Sacra (*see p44*), and to
the north, with its façade covered in
ecstatic saints, is the Jesuit Colégio
Church (*see pp38–9*). To the west is the
Bar O Leque, a good spot for coffee,
shaded by a huge cucumber tree
(*Kigelia africana*).

*Once refreshed you might like to continue
on to the* Elegant Mansions *walk detailed
on pp66–7.*

Walk: Elegant Mansions

The main purpose of the route is to track down the best of Madeira's ornate town houses, but with plenty of other distractions along the way. (*The route is marked in green on the To the Waterfront walk map, pp58–9.*)

Allow 30 minutes for the walk – half a day or more if you visit all the churches and museums along the route.

Start in Praça do Município and walk east out of the square, along Rua C Pestana. Cross Avenida Zarco into Rua da Carreira.

1 Rua da Carreira

This is one of Funchal's most interesting streets, lined with ornate buildings. The predominant colours are white, grey and green – olive green for the pretty wrought-iron balconies and the louvred shutters designed to exclude the searing sun, grey for the carved stone door and window

Delicate patterns wrought from iron

surrounds, and white for the plastered house façades. Most of the owners keep to this colour scheme, but the effect is far from monotonous because every building is different and some have exuberant displays of plants on their balconies.

Three doors to the left is the Patio complex and the **Museu Photographia Vicentes** (Photography Museum) which is currently closed with no signs of reopening anytime in the immediate future. Do continue into the courtyard as there are some good English books shops and an open-air shaded café. Further up on the left, at No. 75, is a baker's shop, noted for its *bolo de mel*, the so-called honey cake, black and dense with nuts and fruit, but actually made with molasses rather than honey. No. 83 has an ancient shop sign declaring itself to be the *Rei das Mobilias* – King of the Furnishers; it sells antique and reproduction furniture. Opposite, No. 102 has a good selection of wickerwork, including baskets, chairs and tables.

Take a look up Rua do Sardo, the next right, which has many more ornate houses. No. 7, on the left, is one of the most plant-filled balconies on the island, a veritable cascade of ferns, geraniums and jade-green succulents.

Back on Rua da Carreira, No. 155 (the local army recruiting office) on the left, is one of the best buildings on the street, with long balconies on both upper floors made of wrought iron in a delicate fan-shaped pattern.

At the next right, Rua do Mouraria, look up to see Nos 3–5, its windows gaily garlanded with floral motifs, somewhat out of keeping with its use as a funeral parlour.

At the next right, you can turn up Rua do Quebra Costas to see the English Church at No. 18, built in the early 19th century, and set in a pretty garden (*see p38*).
Continuing up Rua da Carreira you will finally reach the iron gates of the British Cemetery (ring for entry) with its moving memorials set in a tranquil bird-filled garden (see also p38). Coming out of the cemetery, turn left, then right into Rua das Cruzes.

2 Rua das Cruzes

Towering above you is the **Castelo de São João de Pico**, the Peak Fort, built between 1580 and 1640 when Madeira (as well as all Portugal) was ruled by Spain. The massive fort is now used by the Portuguese Admiralty as a radio station, and so is closed to the public.
*Follow Rua das Cruzes round to the right – you will pass a dull apartment block on the left, then a dignified house on the right that serves as the headquarters of Madeira's Ministry of Forestry, Agriculture and Fisheries. Bear right where the road divides to avoid the traffic, then climb the steps to the left and walk up to the terrace shaded by a huge Indian fig tree (*Ficus benjamina*). From here*

Far-reaching views open up as you reach the end of this walk

there are good views over the English Church and out to the sea. Continue on beneath the walls of the Quinta das Cruzes, the lovely 17th-century villa and garden built on the site where Zarco, Madeira's discoverer, had his house (see p52). Turn right here, down Calçada Santa Clara.

3 Calçada Santa Clara

Santa Clara church (*see p34*) is where Zarco is buried. From here, continue down the steep road past the Museu Frederico de Freitas, another fascinating and elegant house open to the public (*see p50*). At the bottom of the hill you will reach São Pedro church. The main attraction of this church, built in 1598 and remodelled in 1748, is the gilded altar surround and the ceiling painted with flowers, including roses, day lilies, Turk's cap lilies and chrysanthemums. To the right of São Pedro, in Rua do Mouraria, is the Museu Municipal (*see pp50–1*).
Opposite São Pedro, Rua das Pretas will take you back to the start point of the walk.

Central Funchal has many fine town houses, most of them built during the 19th century. The grandest are known as *quintas*, roughly translated as 'mansion' or 'manor house'. Rural *quintas* are usually set in extensive grounds and are connected with some form of agriculture, such as wine production. In the town, *quinta* was simply the name given to the residence of a wealthy or prominent citizen. The dominant architectural style is Baroque, but here there is a very restrained version of this often theatrical style. Door and window surrounds are usually carved into curvaceous shapes but the black-grey basalt used as building stone is too hard for elaborate moulding. Instead, the city's architects achieved their impact through colour, contrasting the soft black of the window and door

frames with the gleaming white of the rendered walls into which they are set. Wrought-iron balconies running the full length of the house ornament smaller houses, many of which are built around a plant-filled patio. Balconies, window shutters, gates and doors are traditionally painted green and the roofs covered in terracotta tiles, so that looking down on the city from above, or approaching by ship, you will see landmark buildings, such as the cathedral tower, pointing a white finger above a sea of warm red. Legislation was passed in 1986 requiring owners to stick to these time-honoured colours, hence the pleasing harmony of the buildings in central Funchal.

Plants and the play of sunlight and shadow add to the delightful variety of Funchal's architecture

Walk: Gardens and Levadas

This walk is designed to provide an introduction to the delights of walking along Madeira's unique irrigation canals, or *levadas (see p136 & pp138–9)*.

You should allow at least two hours for just the walk, an entire day if you want to spend time in the gardens. The gardens Quinta da Boa Vista, Quinta do Palheiro, Quinta do Pomar and Jardim Botanico are located on a very steep hillside, which will make for strenuous walking. You might consider taking a bus or taxi up to the gardens, and enjoy the view on an easier walk down.

The walk is manageable if you are physically fit, do not suffer from vertigo, and are accustomed to walking and climbing steep inclines. A must is a pair of well-proven walking shoes with a good grip for muddy areas. Consider using a walking stick to help take weight off your back and knees, wear light clothing, a hat, sun block and bring water. It is not a good idea to walk the *levadas* alone, go with a group or a knowledgeable tour guide recommended by the tourist office.

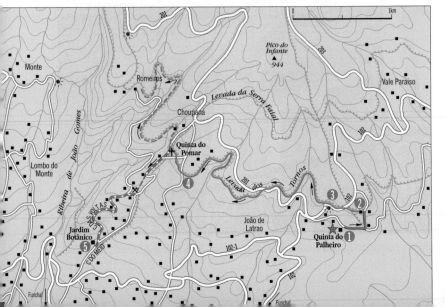

1 Quinta do Palheiro

The walk begins at the Quinta do Palheiro (formerly known as Blandy's Gardens, *see pp102–4*), located 8km northeast of Funchal and reached by bus 37 or taxi. The garden is only open mornings Monday to Friday so start out reasonably early if you want to explore.

2 Levada dos Tornos

This *levada* will take you to the Jardim Botânico (Botanical Garden). To get to the *levada*, turn right out of the Quinta do Palheiro gates, and follow the straight road running alongside the *quinta* wall. At the top of the hill (after 400m) is a junction with a couple of cafés: turn left and walk up the slope. At the crest, turn left to follow a side wall of the white Ramazotti warehouse, with the sports stadium high up on your right: the *levada* starts behind the warehouse. *Following the* levada *footpath you will come to a viewpoint on the left, located on top of the flat roof of the local school.*

3 Viewpoint

The *levada* path passes through a mimosa wood and shortly afterwards meets the EN102 road – a spot whose scruffiness is rescued by the sweeping view over Funchal. This is an urban *levada* and some early stretches have rather more litter and noise than you would want to encounter – it does, however, soon get much better. Cross the road and continue on the *levada* path through pine and mimosa woods, with wonderful views to the left of the Quinta do Palheiro and the golf course. *Continue for 1km until you meet the EN201 road.*

4 To the Quinta do Pomar

Crossing the EN201 you will come to the most enchanting part of the walk as the *levada* twists and turns through a eucalyptus wood, heading up a narrow valley and back along the other side.

You are now well away from roads and the woods are silent except for the sound of running water and the song of birds. Enjoy this idyll while it lasts for you will return to 'civilisation' after 15 minutes of walking. Cross the tarmac road and walk past a *levada* station where the flow of the waters is controlled. Shortly after you will reach the Quinta do Pomar; take the cobbled track on the right, then go left, behind the *quinta* and its little Neo-Gothic chapel. Return to the *levada* path and out, through a red iron door in the *quinta's* garden wall. From here, it is a steep 15-minute walk down to the Botanical Garden. You can, if you prefer, cross the road and continue along the *levada* path for another 15 minutes to the village of Romeiros; here you can catch bus 29 past the Botanical Garden on its way to Funchal.

5 Jardim Botânico

To get to the Botanical Garden (*see pp40–1*) from here, turn left and follow the steep cobbled road downhill. Where the main road swings left, carry straight on down the path for a bird's-eye view of Funchal. At the next junction, the Restaurante Miranda offers a break for coffee. Turn right here, then take the first left down Caminho dos Voltas. After 10 minutes this leads to the Botanical Garden entrance. There are taxis here for the return trip to Funchal, or take buses 29, 30 or 31.

Terraces and Crops

The island of Madeira is a human artefact, shaped and sculpted by African slaves until slavery was abolished in 1775, and then by hardworking islanders engaged in backbreaking toil. Tumultuous geological forces formed the island's deep ravines and hidden valleys, but human hands moulded the slopes into stepped terraces, piling up boulders to create retaining walls. Baskets laden with red-brown soil were carried up from the valley bottom – returning the soil that had been eroded by floods and rain after the early settlers had burned down the tree cover. Little by little the shape of the island was subtly changed, especially on the sunny southern side where the rocks and cliffs absorb sun by day, giving out warmth at night like a radiator. Here, from sea level up to 300m, every patch of cultivable land is used to grow bananas exported in quantity to mainland Portugal, grapes for wine and for eating, and exotic fruits such as mangoes, avocados, passion fruits and papayas. Higher up, market gardeners produce cabbages, carrots, onions, potatoes and yams in tiny fields interspersed by orchards devoted to citrus fruits, custard apples and figs. Higher still, at 400m to 700m, it is common to see fruit trees, such as

apples, pears, plums and cherries, a delightful sight when in blossom in spring. The fruits are used to make *ginja* (cherry liqueur), *sidra* (cider) and other warming distillations, as well as being sold in Funchal's market. Few edible crops are grown above 700m in the woodland zone and this is the point at which the terracing usually stops; even so, good use is made of the fertile volcanic soil for growing eucalyptus, the island's most important timber crop, willows for weaving

and bay trees for flavouring beef *espetada*.

Above left and right: Madeiran terracing, a monument to human perseverance
Below left and right: The fruits of year-long toil

Excursions from Funchal

Moving out of the capital, Funchal, the island is dotted with places awaiting discovery. Visitors have a chance to explore the dramatic terrain and exotic vegetation, whether inland or on the shoreline, and to witness the many faces of traditonal Madeira.

The ubiquitous banana

Boca da Encumeada

The Encumeada Pass is famous for its views, but it really is pot luck whether the views will be of clouds or of deep green valleys at the time of your visit. The pass is at an altitude of 1,007m, and the clouds tend to hang at the 800m level, so you may be bathed in sunshine even if the view below is obscured. On a clear day you can see the sparkling blue seas of the south coast, and then turn round 180 degrees to see the wilder grey seas of the north. To the west is the flat top of the Paúl da Serra plateau and to the east are the great peaks and ridges of the central mountain range. The steep-sided valleys that lead up to the pass from the south and the north are lush, green and intensively cultivated. Together they form a deep cleft that seems almost to cut the island in two. If you want to linger for a while, try

Madeira's appearance changes constantly with the weather

Looking up to Cabo Girão

following one of the *levadas* that radiate out from the pass. The best is the **Levada das Rabaças** which starts opposite (south of) the restaurant and bar. Wild flowers abound on the first part of the route and there are splendid views to the south. You can continue for 15 minutes or so, to the point where the *levada* divides (the right-hand branch goes into a tunnel with a door). Beyond this point there is less to see; the hillsides are slowly recovering from the destructive forest fires of the early 1990s.
On the 104 road, midway between Ribeira Brava and São Vincente, 43km northwest of Funchal.

Cabo Girão

Cabo Girão is one of the most heavily promoted sights on Madeira, billed as the second highest sea cliff in Europe and one of the highest in the world. Guides tend to be rather vague if you ask which is Europe's highest cliff. Pedantic questions are silenced by the truly impressive views down an almost sheer drop to the Atlantic, 580m below. The name of the headland means 'Cape of the Turning', not because the view makes your head spin, but because Zarco sailed this far on his first exploratory trip to Madeira before turning back to Funchal, where he put down his anchor and decided to land. Those who can bear to look down the cliff face for very long will notice that there are tiny terraces dug into the face. It scarcely seems credible that anyone would dare cultivate such tiny and vertiginous plots, and yet the warmth of the south-facing cliffs has tempted some brave farmers to plant vines, flowers and vegetables.
On the south coast, 22km west of Funchal.

Calheta

Bathed in sunshine, Calheta is the main village of a sprawling district that thrives on horticulture; its houses with their pretty gardens seem lost in a sea of bananas and vines. Steep cobbled streets lead down to the coast and several of the region's churches have 16th-century features; they include the Chapel of Our Lady of Loreto on the western outskirts of Arco da Calheta, Calheta's own church, with its fine wooden ceiling, and the Reis Magos Chapel at Estreito da Calheta.

One of the most colourful festivals on the island takes place here on 7 and 8 September, when celebrations for the grape harvest and for Our Lady of Loreto become the excuse for decorating the streets with flowers, setting off noisy fireworks and enjoying beef *espetadas*.
On the south coast, 62km west of Funchal.

The Grape Harvest

The grape harvest lasts far longer on Madeira than in other wine-producing regions of Europe because the fruit ripens at different times, depending upon the altitude.

The harvest is a family affair and the pickers set to work from the middle to the end of August. They start with the sweet grape varieties, grown on the lower slopes, and work upwards to the sercial vines, grown for the driest wines, at around 700m. They then return to sea level to end the harvest in early November, picking the muscatel grapes whose sugars have now been concentrated by the sun. If you are travelling round Madeira in the autumn it is difficult to miss the trucks laden with grapes bound for the factories of Madeira's leading wine producers; local people cannot wait the 20 years or so that it takes to produce fine Madeira,

though, and a certain amount of the harvest goes into the production for purely local consumption of fruity wines such as *canina* (from Estreito de Câmara de Lobos), *jaquet* (from Seixal and Porto Moniz) and *americana* (from Porto da Cruz). A little of this wine is still produced the traditional way, for old times' sake, by treading the grapes in a stone or cement tank called a *lagar*. Most of the grapes, however, are put through a stainless steel, electric-powered press. The juice is placed in barrels and left to ferment – local wine is drunk very young and the first batch will be ready for tasting in early November, coinciding with the end of the harvest. Now everyone can relax and enjoy the fruit of their labour.

Visitors to Madeira can enjoy the fruits without the hard work – Funchal hosts a month-long wine festival in September, which is

good fun, even if it is put on *para o inglês ver* (literally 'for the eyes of the English', that is, for the benefit of tourists). For a taste of the real thing, head for Estreito de Câmara de Lobos,

20km west of Funchal, the island's vineyard capital – here you can watch the harvest and take your pick from a number of bars and restaurants serving the local wines.

Madeiran grapes represent a major source of income and are picked with care

Madeiran wickerwork on display in Camacha

Camacha

Camacha is a village devoted to the production and sale of wickerwork. Almost everyone who lives here is employed in the industry, either as weaver or as vendor. The main building on the village square is the Café Relogio (Clock Café), a multi-storey emporium crammed with wickerwork and often crowded with coach-borne shoppers. Here you can see a vast range of wickerwork products, from tea trays, plant-pot holders and magazine racks, to peacock-backed chairs, bedheads and picture frames – enough, in fact, to furnish every part of the house if you were so minded. Most visitors content themselves with modest purchases – a shopping basket or gardener's trug, for example, which are easier to carry home by air. The shop will arrange freight

forwarding for larger items if you wish, but the prices can be steep for bulky items. If you are lucky, you will be able to watch willow weavers at work in the supermarket basement. They work with extraordinary speed, the result of years of practice. Most weavers specialise in one type of wickerwork – be it linen baskets or babies' cradles – and build up a proficiency over time. Just for fun, and to show off their artistic skills, a group of local weavers created a vast galleon, with billowing sails, and a Noah's Ark, with elephants, lions, monkeys and deer, which is displayed on the middle floor. None of these are for sale, a fact which disappoints some visitors. The Café Relogio (Largo Achada, *tel: (291) 922777*) above the wicker warehouse is the venue for folk nights every Saturday evening when the local dance group, one of the best on the island, gives a spirited performance.

15km northeast of Funchal.

Câmara de Lobos

Sir Winston Churchill, the British wartime Prime Minister, is regarded with almost saintly reverence on Madeira because he helped to put the island on the tourist map. From 1949 he made regular visits to paint the local landscape and, in particular, the little fishing village of Câmara de Lobos. Now a plaque on the wall alongside the busy 101 road east of the harbour marks the spot where Churchill sat to paint the view, and local shops sell rather fuzzy black and white postcards of the great man at work, unmistakable with his trademark cigar and panama hat. It is interesting to speculate how much the fishing village has changed since Churchill's day. It looks as pretty as ever, with gaily painted boats drawn up on the tiny pebble beach. The tiny harbourside houses are painted in the same bright colours – primary red, yellow, blue and green against brilliant white. Yet there is an air of distressing poverty about the place as well – this is about the only village on Madeira where you are likely to be pestered by begging children, and the streets running down to the harbour smell of more than just the detritus of the fishing industry. The fishermen here work all night to catch *espada* fish which are then sold in the harbourside wholesale market. You will have to come very early to see this in operation, since most of the trading is over by 7am. The busiest place in the village then becomes the nearby bar, where the profits from a hard night's work can be easily gambled and drunk away. A tiny chapel in the bar district hints at the hardships of the fishing life: scenes from the life of St Nicholas, patron saint of seafarers, include vivid depictions of shipwrecks and drownings.

8km west of Funchal.

Discussing the catch at the fishing village of Câmara de Lobos

Wickerwork

Wickerwork is one of Madeira's most important cottage industries, employing some 2,500 people. The industry dates back to the 19th century when cane furniture was very popular and Madeirans began copying examples imported to the island by

British visitors. Today the wicker products sold as souvenirs represent only a fraction of the island's total output, most of which is exported to the USA and Europe.

Willows are grown all over the island at heights of 700–800m, where the cloud tends to hang, providing plenty of moisture. The trees are pollarded by having all their branches cut off at a relatively young age. This encourages the tree to produce lots of new shoots which can grow up to 2m in length in a single growing season. The shoots are harvested from January to March and left to soak in water before the bark is peeled off. They are then dried, often by being exposed to the sun on the roofs of willow weavers' houses. Before being woven into baskets or furniture, the canes are

boiled to make them supple, which turns their colour from white to the more familiar brown. Walking around the countryside, you may well see great bundles of willow stacked in the sun, and you may even see weavers at work, seated on low stools outside their houses.

Demonstrations of willow weaving can be seen at Camacha (*p78*), the centre of the industry, where you can also marvel at the bewildering array of different wicker products – from simple place mats to the most ornate bird cages.

Willow weavers display their dexterity and skill

Caniçal

Caniçal is a gritty little working port where the fishing community gets on with its business as if the tourists were invisible. Most visitors come here for the Museu da Baleia (Whale Museum) but then find themselves drawn to the nearby beach where it is possible to stand around for an hour or more, watching the boat builders at work or the tuna fishermen bringing in their catch. It takes less time to view the museum itself, which contains an endearingly jumbled exhibition on the theme of the whale – sculptures, old engravings, ancient and modern scrimshaw carved from whale ivory, a lifesize wax model of a sperm whale, 12m long, and a whaling boat of similar length. What is not immediately apparent is that this museum is conservationist in outlook – you have to watch the museum video to realise this.

The rather slow-moving 45-minute documentary reveals how marine conservationists are tapping into the memories and experiences of retired Madeiran whale fishermen, many of them based in Caniçal, in order to understand more about the movements and habits of the sperm whale. Their comments, along with readings from Herman Melville's whaling classic, *Moby Dick* (1851), provide an informative commentary to the film itself, which shows scientists tracking a school of whales in the seas between Madeira and the Azores, filming them at play, feeding and even reproducing. The video shows that very little is known about these endangered whales and their movements, but it is hoped that they will find a sanctuary off the coast of Madeira in the newly established marine reserves (*see pp130–1*).

To the east of Caniçal you can see the building that once served as Madeira's principal whaling station, where whale carcasses were reduced to ivory, oil and ambergris (the waxy lining of the whales' intestines, used in perfume manufacture). Now the building is part of the much bigger free port (Zona Franca) complex, intended to attract overseas investment funds and manufacturing to Madeira.

32km east of Funchal. Museu da Baleia open: Tue–Sun 10am–6pm.

Caniço's church, an architectural masterpiece in grey and white

Caniço

Caniço is worth a brief visit for its

imposing 18th-century Baroque church, whose tall bell tower is visible to all motorists as they speed along the road from Funchal to the airport.

Some 2km southeast, on the coast at Caniço de Baixa, is the **Roca Mar** resort complex, noted for its diving facilities: there is good diving off the beach here and at the nearby underwater nature park, 4km west at **Ponta do Garajau**. Literally translated, Ponta do Garajau means 'Tern Point' – so named because early explorers found a large colony of terns nesting on the cliffs below. Today its most prominent feature is a statue of Christ with outstretched arms, smaller than similar statues in Rio de Janeiro and Lisbon, and erected in 1927. The headland commands good views of Funchal, and the sunset can be dazzlingly colourful. If you decide that you want to linger, you can eat back in Caniço, where there is a good choice of several popular restaurants and bars

The sailors' friend: statue of the Redeemer on the coast at Ponta do Garajau

catering to locals and to the German visitors who favour the nearby resorts. *9km east of Funchal.*

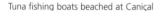

Tuna fishing boats beached at Caniçal

Curral das Freiras

Curral das Freiras means Nuns' Refuge, or Valley of the Nuns. The name derives from the fact that the nuns of Santa Clara convent (*see p34*) fled here in 1566 to escape from pirates who were attacking the city. The green and unspoilt valley retains a sense of remoteness and other-worldliness even now, despite the number of visitors who come here. It takes half a day to make the excursion, which illustrates how the mountainous terrain of Madeira can magnify distances.

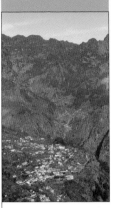

Curral das Freiras or Valley of the Nuns

The best route out of Funchal is to head westwards along the Estrada Monumental (101 road), passing through the Hotel Zone, then heading north on the 105. The first part of the journey is not very promising, as the road winds through the western suburbs of Funchal, past untidy housing estates, an army base and the clusters of satellite dishes used by the island's telecommunications authority.

São Martinho
Stopping off at São Martinho, you can take in the fine views from the terrace in front of the massive modern church (built 1930–52). Inside, in a room to the right of the main altar, is a small museum which doubles as a Sunday school. The exhibits include a silver processional cross and 18th-century garments, embroidered in gold, made for dressing up the religious statues on special feast days.

Pico dos Barcelos
From São Martinho northwards the views improve as you climb to this second viewpoint, located at 364m; several restaurants with terraces have been built here to take advantage of the views back to Funchal. Beyond this peak, take the 107 road (marked on some maps as the 203), following the narrow winding road to Curral das Freiras as it climbs to the eastern side of the Socorridos valley, passing through eucalyptus woods.

Eira do Serrado
Before descending to Curral das Freiras, it is worth diverting to this 'eagle's nest' or eyrie, to look down on the village which forms the end point of the journey. To reach the viewpoint, you first have to walk through a scruffy car park where stallholders will try to sell you T-shirts or locally made *ginja* (cherry liqueur). Once through this barrage, you follow a path through sweet chestnut woods which are alive with dancing butterflies when the trees are in flower. The view from the *miradouro* is breathtaking and it reveals

why some guides describe the valley as a crater – from this position you get the impression of being on the edge of a great cauldron, completely surrounded by towering cliffs and jagged peaks. This natural amphitheatre magnifies the sounds so well that you can hear every dog bark and cock crow in the tiny village far down below.

Curral das Freiras

The final descent to the village follows a road that was not built until 1959 and which passes through several rock-cut tunnels. The old footpath linking the village to the outside world still exists, wide and grassy, zigzagging down the hillside – you can see the start of the path on the left after you emerge from the first tunnel. Once in the village the traditional thing to do, especially if you have walked all the way, is take coffee and eat the local speciality, warm chestnut bread, in one of the bars on the narrow main square. The Nuns' Valley Restaurant is regarded as the best bar – perhaps because the owner makes and sells his own *licor de castanha*, a liqueur which tastes like chestnut-flavoured gin, which he sells by the bottle or glass. If you come here on a Sunday there will normally be a street market in full swing. If not, you can walk on down the main street to the bottom of the valley and enjoy the peace of this favoured spot, basking in the sunshine and surrounded by dramatic scenery.
20km north of Funchal.

Locked away in its own secret valley is the Nuns' Refuge that is now a thriving village

Machico

After Funchal, Machico is Madeira's second largest town, with a population of 13,000. The town is divided by the River Machico and sits at the mouth of a fertile green valley backed by mountains. The intensively cultivated terraces clinging to the valley sides show that many local people make their living in agriculture, while there is a small boatyard and fishing harbour on the coast. With the building of the Oasis Atlantic and Dom Pedro hotels on the western side of the town, Machico has begun to develop as a tourist resort.

Machico's small harbour
has a fertile hinterland

Some say that Machico is named after Robert Machin (*see pp14–15*), the English sailor who was shipwrecked on Madeira with his companions before the island was officially claimed by Portugal. Zarco is said to have found Machin's grave, marked by a rough cross of cedarwood, when he first landed. Others say that Zarco was moved by homesickness to name the spot after his native town of Monchique on mainland Portugal. Once settlement of the island got under way, Zarco ruled the western part from Funchal, and his fellow navigator, Tristão Vaz Teixeira, as Captain General of the eastern part, ruled from Machico.

Machico is 24km northeast of Funchal.

Igreja Matriz

Teixeira's statue stands in the town's main square, in front of the Igreja Matriz, the parish church of Machico. Though less ornate than Funchal's cathedral, this church is of similar vintage, founded at the end of the 15th century under the patronage of King Manuel I of Portugal and with a handsome Gothic portal.

Cristo Chapel

Older still is the Cristo Chapel, built, according to tradition, on the site of Robert Machin's grave soon after Zarco landed on this spot. Floods have frequently damaged the chapel, which has been rebuilt numerous times, most recently in 1957. Locals call it the Capela dos Milagres (Chapel of Miracles) after the miracle-working crucifix inside – though its miraculous powers are now rarely sought since the chapel is often locked. The crucifix lived up to its reputation in 1803 when floods devastated the chapel. Not long afterwards, an American sailor landed on Madeira bearing the cross – he had spotted the image floating on the waves and was eventually able to return it to the rebuilt chapel. The crucifix is carried round the town in a torchlight procession on the nights of 8 and 9 October.

Forte do Amparo and Pico do Facho
Not far from the chapel is the triangular Forte do Amparo, built in 1708 near the seafront to provide Machico with some measure of defence against pirate raids. So devastating were these raids that a constant lookout was kept from the hill to the north of the town, known as the Pico do Facho (Torch Peak). Warning bonfires or beacons were lit if danger threatened, and this practice is remembered every year on the last Sunday in August when a huge bonfire is lit to celebrate the Festa do Santissimo Sacramento (Feast of the Holy Sacrament). Pico do Facho is easy to reach by road from Machico: take the Caniçal road and turn left just before the entrance to the road tunnel. There are fine views from the summit, with Santa Catarina airport, 4km to the southwest, prominent in the foreground and the cliffs of Ponta do São Lourenço in the opposite direction.

Machico's fishing fleet stands ready for a long night at sea

Already burgeoning: the recently created Monte Palace Tropical Garden

Monte

The twin-towered church of Nossa Senhora do Monte is a prominent landmark high on the hillside above Funchal. To devout Madeiran Catholics, the church is a constant reminder of Virgin Mary's protective role as the island's patron saint. To visitors, Monte means something quite different – a chance to glide up to the town by the new cable car and return by the famous Monte toboggan ride, which many consider to be the highlight of their trip.

Monte stands at 550m above sea level and the steep uphill journey used to be made by rack-and-pinion railway. This opened in 1893 and carried visitors from Funchal up the hillside, past the colourful gardens of numerous rural villas and mansions, to the station at Monte, taking 20 minutes to make the climb. Disaster struck in 1919 when one of the boilers of the steam locomotive exploded, killing four people and injuring many more. From then on, visitors and locals alike turned their back on the railway, regarding it as a dangerous means of transport. The company struggled on until 1939, when the railway was closed and the line dismantled.

Monte Gardens

A short stretch of elevated viaduct survives from the old railway and this is the first sight that greets today's visitors arriving by car or bus. The station building survives on the shady main square, Largo do Fonte, as does the station garden, first laid out in 1894. The rather formal outlines of this garden have now been softened by the rampant green creepers that have cloaked the railway bridge in green and pushed out tendrils to spiral up the trunks of the tree ferns, obviously thriving in Monte's humid climate. A short way south of this public garden is the entrance to the Monte Palace Tropical Garden (Caminho do Monte 174), a relatively new arrival but one which promises to be the best on Madeira as it approaches maturity – the 7 hectares of hillside surrounding the Monte Palace have been skilfully planted with areas devoted to Madeiran flora, oriental species, azaleas, ferns and orchids.

Nossa Senhora do Monte (Our Lady of Monte)

For a breathtaking ride to **Monte** take the cable car which ascends from (and descends to) Funchal's Zona Velha (Old Town). See Funchal fade away in the distance on this 10-minute glass cable car ride. You will arrive in Monte at Largo das Barboses a short walk to the **Monte Palace Tropical Garden**, or you can take the new (2005) cable car from

Monte connecting to the garden. This 7-minute trip affords beautiful views of Funchal's bay and the João Gomes River. It also provides walkers easier access to the *levada* walks of **Tomos, Bom Sucesso** and **Curral dos Romeiros**.

An extreme and thrilling way to descend back to Funchal is via the historic toboggan ride (*see p91*); white-suited drivers wait for passengers at the foot of the steps leading to the Monte church.

Devout pilgrims who visit Monte will climb the 74 steep steps of the church on their knees. The handsome church stands on the site of a chapel built in 1470 by Adam Gonçalves Ferreira. He and his twin sister Eve were the first children born on Madeira. The church was rebuilt in Baroque style following an earthquake, and re-dedicated in 1818. Inside, in a silver tabernacle above the altar, is a precious statue of the Virgin which is carried in procession on the Feast of the Assumption. More imposing is the black coffin chest in the chapel to the left (north) of the nave which contains the mortal remains of the Emperor Charles I, the last in the long line of Hapsburg emperors. Crowned Emperor of Austria and King of Hungary in 1916, he was deposed in 1918 and exiled first to Switzerland and then, at his own request, to Madeira. He did not live long on the island, dying of a sudden attack of pneumonia in 1922, aged 35, leaving a wife and several children.

6km north of Funchal. Monte Palace Tropical Garden open: Mon–Fri 9am–6pm, Sat 9am–5pm. Admission charge. Monte church open: daily 9.30am–1pm & 3–6pm.

Pilgrims climb on their knees to visit Monte's revered church

Terreiro da Luta

On the hillside just above Monte is the spot known as Terreiro da Luta, marked by a statue of the Virgin standing on top of a 5.5-m high column. It was in this spot that the little statue of the Virgin, revered in the church at Monte, appeared miraculously to a shepherd girl in the 15th century. The present statue dates to 1927, when it was erected in fulfilment of a vow made by devout Madeirans during the bombardment of Funchal by a German submarine in 1916. During World War I the Germans sought to end Madeira's use as a supply base for Atlantic shipping by sending in a submarine which first sank a number of ships moored in Funchal's harbour and then shelled the city itself. Appealing to the Virgin of Monte for protection, pilgrims promised to erect a statue in her honour. The bombardment ceased and Funchal survived the rest of the war unscathed, so grateful Madeirans created the present memorial. Round the foot of the monument is a symbolic rosary, made from the anchor chains salvaged from Allied ships sunk in the harbour by German torpedoes.

A short step away from the monument is the terminus of the defunct Funchal to Monte railway (see p88). The palatial station building, which opened in 1912, also served as a restaurant. Today it continues to be used for receptions and functions.

Passengers visiting Madeira on luxury cruise liners are often brought here for cocktails and to enjoy the expansive views down over the grey-green heads of fragrant eucalyptus trees to the red roofs of Funchal, some 876m below. It is then *de rigueur* to make the descent back to Funchal by toboggan, a method of transport that has thrilled and intrigued visitors to Madeira for nearly 150 years. If you do not want to make the trip, the toboggan drivers, dressed in traditional straw hat and white flannels, will usually let you take their photograph in return for a small tip.

The Virgin of Monte, invoked to protect Funchal from war-time bombardment

The Monte Toboggan

Hemingway, not a man given to expressing strong emotions, described the toboggan ride from Monte to Funchal as one of the most exhilarating experiences of his life. Sliding in a wicker basket on wooden runners over the polished cobbles, toboggans can at times reach considerable speeds, though the drivers, with their rubber soled boots for grip, ensure that corners are negotiated safely. Sadly, the high cost of maintaining cobbled roads is encouraging the increased use of tarmac and the descent of the toboggans over certain sections of the run is becoming perceivably slower as a result.

Madeiran tobogganing as a method of transport was invented in 1850, it is said,

though horse- and bullock-drawn sleds were in use for transport well before that date. Some visitors consider this the essential Madeiran experience, but it does not come cheap. You can go all the way to Funchal on a 4km ride, lasting 20 minutes, for around €11 per person (two people per sled), or take the shorter run to Livramento (2km; 10 minutes) for €7 per person. You will, though, be expected to tip the drivers, and pay for the rather blurred polaroid photograph that the driver's colleague will take along the route, expecting to sell it to you as a souvenir at the end of your brief journey.

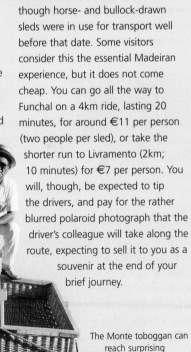

The Monte toboggan can reach surprising speeds

Paúl da Serra

As if to prove that Madeira is not one vast floating flower garden, the Paúl da Serra looms bleakly to the eastern end of the island. The name Paúl da Serra means 'Desert Plain', a very apt description for the high plateau where the soil is so thin that only the toughest of grasses will grow.

Even this is cropped tight by goats, sheep and sturdy little cows, and their numbers are strictly limited to prevent all the vegetation from being consumed. Travelling across the plain to Rabaçal or Porto Moniz, you will see caves dug into the sides of embankments to provide shelter for the farmers and for their beasts. You will also see their more modern, but substantially less aesthetic, equivalent, large concrete sheds. Shelter

is necessary because it is often very windy up on top of the plateau and this is where the snow will fall, if at all, during the winter months.

A forest of wind turbines has recently been built on the plateau to provide electricity to settlements along the island's north coast, the gleaming white towers and propeller blades looking very high-tech and modern in contrast to the elemental moorland. It is not always wet, windy or misty up here, however, and in summer people come here to camp, play football in the big flat open spaces, and look for the delicious fruits of the bilberry.

The Paúl da Serra also plays a vital role in the island's irrigation system. Rainwater is captured and channelled into reservoirs from which it is fed into

The unexpectedly flat expanse of moorland on Madeira's high plateau

power stations and *levadas*. The volcanic rock of the Paúl da Serra also acts as a huge sponge, absorbing rainfall which then filters down through the porous substrata until it meets layers of impermeable clay at around the 1,000m level. Here the water pours out of the ground, sometimes to cascade as spectacular waterfalls (at Rabaçal, for example, *see p120*) but more often to feed the island's extensive *levada* network (*see pp138–9*).
60km northwest of Funchal.

Madeira's highest peaks are linked by knife-edge ridges and plunging cliffs

Pico do Arieiro

At 1,810m, this is Madeira's third highest mountain peak, and its most accessible (*see pp124–5 for a* walk). You can drive from the centre of Funchal to the top in little under an hour. Just before the peak, you will pass a small round-roofed ice house on the left, built in 1800 to store compressed snow which supplied Funchal's hotels with ice in the days before refrigeration. Snow is a relatively rare occurrence. Most of the time visitors bask in bright sunshine, high above the rainclouds, enjoying views that stretch across the whole of the island. Connoisseurs of the night sky and the dawn light say that you have not lived until you have spent a night on the mountain to view the Milky Way and the shooting stars that rain down in the early hours of the morning, followed by the most spectacular sunrise. Fortunately you do not have to rough it to spend a night on the mountain. The government-owned *pousada* (guesthouse and restaurant), just below the summit, provides every modern luxury.
23km north of Funchal.

Pico Ruivo

Just as spectacular is the sunrise viewed from Madeira's highest peak, the 1,862m Pico Ruivo. Unfortunately, this mountain summit is much less accessible but you can walk to it along the well-marked path from its smaller neighbour, **Pico do Arieiro** (*see pp124–5*), provided that you have a head for heights and the time (allow 3 hours each way). Alternatively, you can drive from Santana to Achada do Teixeira, and walk the final stretch up the eastern flank of the mountain (allow 45 minutes each way). There are glorious views over the northeastern coast along the route and from the peak.
45km north of Funchal via Santana.

Standing on the top of Pico do Arieiro, the view in every direction is of classic volcanic rock formations, enough to send a geologist into paroxysms of excitement. Even to the non-specialist the parched, sponge-like rocks in spectacular colours such as purple, orange, chocolate and red speak of tumultuous volcanic events. The central mountains of Madeira are made up of solidified lava and ash which began to form beneath the sea in the Miocene Era, 20 million years ago, gradually building up until the lava broke the water's surface, forming a small conical island. Further eruptions then spilled lava down the eastern and western flanks, resulting in the present elongated shape. Massive earth movements also played a part, tilting, squeezing and crushing the layers of solid rock, so that you can see cliffs on Pico do Arieiro where different coloured strata are squashed and folded into bizarre concertina shapes. Hot lava continued to push through joints, gaps and weak points in the rock, so that you will also see great columns and beds of hard basalt interlayered with softer tufas and compressed ash. When all the volcanic activity ceased about 1.7 million years ago, the weathering began – rain and river erosion created the island's spectacular ravines and knife-edge

ridges cutting deep into the weakest, softest rocks and leaving the hard rock still standing.

As a result Madeira now consists of a central spine, composed of lofty mountains, the remains of the original volcanic peaks, and numerous deep valleys running off to the north and south, lush with the dense vegetation that Madeira's climate and the fertile soil combine to support.

Dawn light enhances the colours of the rocks on Madeira's high peaks

Fragrant eucalyptus, introduced from Australia as a source of timber

Poiso

The pass at Poiso is a favourite stopping-off point for walkers and travellers exploring the high peaks of the island's interior because the Abrigo do Poiso restaurant on the crossroads is a welcoming place, with a log fire to comfort chilled or wet bodies. The same fire is used for grilling delicious beef *espetadas*. Poiso sits on the eastern edge of the **Montado do Barreiro National Park**, an area of woodland and open moors, threaded by a tortuously winding narrow road (only open 8am to 7pm). Experiments in reafforestation are being carried out here to give this part of Madeira back its original wooded outline and produce commercially valuable timber. Maritime pine, eucalyptus (Tasmanian blue gum), Douglas fir, Lawson cypress, Japanese red cedar and Indian silver fir are the principal trees being planted. Wild ponies, wild boar and rabbits are found here – all said to be the descendants of animals imported by early settlers. Rabbits have become such a nuisance that hunting is allowed on Thursdays and Sundays in September, October and November – it is best not to wander off the beaten track on these occasions because of the danger of stray shots. Barbecue pits, spring-water taps and picnic tables are scattered round the park, and on summer weekends Madeirans love to come here to camp.

Small patches of natural Madeiran vegetation can be found within the remoter valleys of the park, a tiny fraction of the dense woodland that covered the island until it was burned and felled by the early colonisers. Madeirans call these patches of indigenous woodland the *lauri silva*, meaning laurel woods. The laurels concerned are the *Laurus azonica*, which is a type of bay tree, and the Canary laurel (*Apollonius barbajuna*), both tough low-growing evergreens with leathery leaves. These are usually found growing in association with the *til* tree (*Ocotea foetens*), whose flowers have a sharp penetrating scent, and the *vinhático* (*Persea indica*), used by the early settlers for furniture making and known as Madeiran mahogany for its colour and hardness.

10km north of Funchal.

Ponta Delgada

Ponta Delgada is a small village on the north coast noted for its tiny harbour and for its willow-tree plantations, which provide the raw material for the island's wickerwork industry. The best time to visit is on the first Sunday in September when the Feast of Senhor Jesus is celebrated and the whole village is decked in festive flowers and greenery. The festival celebrates an ancient crucifix which was washed ashore here in the 16th century. Believing it to be miraculous, the local people built a chapel to house the crucifix but a fire destroyed the building and consumed most of the cross in 1908. Undeterred, the villages rebuilt the church and they still revere the charred cross fragments, which are displayed in a glass case for most of the year.

27km west of Santana on the north coast, 60km from Funchal.

Ponta do Pargo

Ponta do Pargo, or Dolphin Point, is the westernmost headland on Madeira: you can walk out to the lighthouse at the tip for views of the coast, knowing that nothing lies beyond this point except Atlantic waves until America is reached.

If you are interested in wild flowers, you should walk the **Levada Nova**, which runs from Ponta do Pargo to Calheta (a distance of 20km, but the 101 road with frequent bus services to Funchal is never very far away if you get tired). The combination of moisture and sunshine ensures that the margins of this *levada* have some of the most varied and colourful flowers to be found on the island.

78km west of Funchal.

The red roofs of Ponta Delgada, sheltered by tree-clad hills

Massive cliffs mark the easternmost tip of
Madeira at Ponta de São Lourenço

Ponta de São Lourenço

The easternmost tip of Madeira does
not dip gracefully down to the sea with
gentle gradient; true to the tumultuous
character of the island's terrain, it stops
abruptly at the precipitous edge of
several canyon-like cliffs 180m or more
above sea level. Atlantic waves pound
the base of the cliffs, undermining them
gradually so that every so often great
rocks crash down to join the smashed
up boulders already littered chaotically
between the cliffs and the sea. If you
could see beneath the waves you would
discover that the Ilhas Desertas, usually
visible offshore to the southeast, are a
continuation of the same basic
geological formations, though separated
by a drowned valley some 100m deep.

For the romantically inclined this is a
spot to savour for its wild and breezy
loneliness (*see pp128–9* for a suggested
walk) but when that palls you can take a
dip in the more protected **Praínha Bay**,
signposted to the south of the 101 road,
midway between Caniçal and the end of
the road. The beach is reached by means
of a steep path near the chapel of Nossa
Senhora de Piedate. Though not large,
this is the only beach on Madeira with
sand – black sand composed of crushed
shells in which you may find tiny
fragments of vegetation fossilised by
volcanic ash.
32km east of Funchal.

Ponta do Sol

Ponta do Sol basks in the sunshine after
which it is named: Sun Point is the last
village travelling westwards along
Madeira's southern coast to receive day-
long sunshine – beyond here, cliffs and
hills cast shadows in the early part of the
day, especially when the sun is low in
winter. Exploiting the sunshine to full
effect, Ponta do Sol is a major centre of
banana cultivation, and there is very
little space around the town not covered
by plantations: even the cliff faces have
tiny terraces which have been hacked
out of them and support a few banana
plants, as you will see if you follow the
coast road – look out for steps cut in the
rock face and precipitous paths leading
to terraces as you approach the tunnel
that leads to Madalena do Mar. The
effort of creating and tending such
terraces is justified by the extra warmth
given out by the rock face at night,
storing sunlight by day and acting as a
radiator. This helps to ripen the crop

sooner in the year, and can mean a premium price if the bananas are ready for sale well before the main crop. Some 600,000kg of bananas are exported from Madeira every year, much of it to Lisbon for sale in mainland Portugal. Ponta do Sol has one of the island's principal packing stations, unmissable because of the stalks piled outside the warehouse beside the main road, waiting to be pulped and processed into animal fodder or glues.

The next-door village of **Madalena do Mar** has an interesting history, for tradition attributes the founding of the village to King Ladislav of Poland. Having been defeated at the Battle of Varna in 1414, Ladislav set off on a

Decorating the streets in preparation for Madeira's June flower festival

pilgrimage round the world, visiting holy sites and doing good wherever he could.

His travels eventually brought him to Madeira, where Zarco, the island's discoverer, persuaded him to settle, granting him the land around Madalena do Mar. He founded Madalena do Mar's little church of Santa Catarina in 1457. Knowing nothing of his history, the locals called him Henrique Alemão, or Henry the German.
42km west of Funchal.

Even the cinema in Ponta do Sol alludes to the sunshine after which the village is named

Porto Moniz

Porto Moniz is located at the remote northwestern tip of Madeira, about as far as you can get from Funchal, so it is not surprising that until not so long ago there were people in the village who had never seen the island's capital. Even today it feels different from other villages on Madeira, although it has rapidly caught up with the modern world and now boasts several hotels, cafés and restaurants, and the island's only official campsite.

Wild seas, sheer cliffs and cascading waterfalls mark the north coast road

The fresh arrival of roads and electricity has given a boost to the village and opened it up to tourism, but for many villagers the old, slow pace of life continues and few of them own vehicles; walking, often with heavy burdens, is still the norm. Road embankments, built or patched up with concrete elsewhere, are masterpieces of drystone walling round here, and they support a rich flora, covered in succulent house leeks and other wall plants.

The tiny fields are meticulously cultivated, as you will see if you look down on the village from above: there is a fine viewpoint to the north of the village on the 101 road. The terraces that tumble down the hillside and the flat fields around the village itself, are all fenced with dried heather and bracken, creating a low 0.5-m boundary wall which is sufficient to protect the crops from the strong Atlantic winds, driving rain and salt-laden sea spray.

Descending into the village, you will find all the paraphernalia of a developing seaside resort, including a go-kart track and shops selling buckets and spades, despite the absence of sand. This is all part of a general diversification scheme to help the villagers reduce their dependence on agriculture.

For many visitors, Porto Moniz is the start or end point of a drive along the spectacular north coast road. It has several excellent seafood restaurants which attract coach parties at lunchtime. For those on a longer stay, there is an unusual swimming pool next to the Residencial Calhau hotel on the edge of the ocean. Natural rock pools in the volcanic rocks have been deepened and linked by concrete pathways: you cannot swim far in the pools, but you can bask in the sun-warmed water while watching the Atlantic waves rolling in and beating against the shore.
75km north west of Funchal.

North Coast Road

You will see more of these mighty waves as you drive the exhilarating north coast road from Porto Moniz to São Vicente (*see pp114–15*). The road is one of those spectacular pieces of construction at which the Madeirans seem to excel – like the island's *levadas*, construction of the road was a slow manual process of hacking away at the stone to create a narrow ledge in the cliff side, sometimes passing through tunnels.

No machinery or modern technology made the task easier, and that is why the road took 16 years to complete, almost one year for each kilometre of its 19-km length.

Drive slowly, because the road is only wide enough for one vehicle in places; watch out for oncoming vehicles and be prepared to pull over into a passing place if necessary. While waiting, you can admire the wild seas, the sheer cliffs and the numerous waterfalls which cascade over them, often soaking your car or – as the Madeirans say – giving you a free car wash.

Dried heather fences protect the tiny fields of Porto Moniz from sea winds

Quinta do Palheiro

Blandy's Gardens

The gardens were first laid out in the 18th century by the original owner, the wealthy Count of Carvalhal, but his heirs proved profligate with their inheritance and the estate was purchased from them by the Blandy family in 1885. Successive generations of the Blandy family have tended the garden, which is an interesting blend of English-style design and tropical planting.

Striking flowers and foliage are guaranteed year round

Of all Madeira's gardens, this one is the most rewarding. If you follow the Gardens and Levadas walk (*pp70–1*), you can combine a morning spent here

Tropical plants add exotic interest to a garden that is essentially English in style

with a visit to Funchal's Jardim Botânico for a day of horticultural indulgence.

If you arrive by car, you can drive from the ticket office at the entrance to the car park by the house, but walkers will enjoy the stroll down the cobbled drive where trees are interspersed with camellias and massed agapanthus line the avenue – and the view to the left is one of hay meadows and woodland, a scene that could almost be in England.

Blandy's Gardens are located 550m above sea level, so it is cool and moist enough for oak, beech and chestnut trees to thrive. These were planted by the Blandy family decades ago to remind them of their English origins.

At the bottom of the drive, signposts direct you to a sunny terrace below the house, hung with scented jasmine, roses and other climbers. In the beds below, butterflies dart about amid colourful salvias and verbenas.

From the centre of the terrace there is a stone staircase, flanked by flame-shaped Italian cypress trees and terracotta urns, which gives a good view of the house (not open to the public).

Below the staircase is a wide path lined with rare and unusual trees, such as the sweet-scented magnolia-like *Michelia doltsopa* and the ancient gnarled *Hagerstromia indica*, a Chinese tree which sheds its bark to reveal fresh colours beneath.

Midway down this central walk, a path to the left leads to a bridge across a frog-filled pond, and to a little chapel built in restrained Baroque style by the Count of Carvalhal.

Beyond the chapel is a magnificent long border modelled on the typical English herbaceous border – but planted with spectacular abutilons, angel's trumpet (*Datura sanguinea*) and other tender plants among the blue delphiniums and multi-coloured sweet peas.

The most beautiful part of the garden comes next: the Ladies' Garden, a serene spot where you can bask in the sunlight while enjoying the birdsong and looking out over hedges clipped to the shape of peahens sitting in their nests. The topiary forms are created out of *Muelenbeckia*, an Australian plant similiar to box, that lends itself well to clipping into intricate designs.

Among the striking plants here is a wonderfully gnarled *Saphora japonica* tree fringed by a cascade of branches sweeping down from the crown to the ground. Another plant is a *Sparmannia africana* whose simple white flowers open to reveal wonderful yellow and scarlet stamens, much visited by bees.

A path to the right of the Ladies' Garden leads out through a low iron

A garden typically English in design and tropical in its planting

gate into a long alley of plane trees and up to the Count of Carvalhal's 18th-century house, which is fronted by giant holm oaks and three deep-water troughs colonised by frogs.

Beyond the house is woodland, and eventually you get back to the formal gardens. A signpost points left towards 'Inferno' (Hell), but far from being hot, the woods are cool, wet, shaded and full of graceful tree ferns and masses of vivid blue trailing morning glory vine. *8km east of Funchal, off the 102 Camacha road. Open: Mon–Fri 9.30am–12.30pm. Admission charge.*

Rabaçal

Rabaçal itself consists of no more than a government resthouse, but the woods around it are among the most scenic on Madeira, supporting an ecological community of ancient laurel and tree heath, and rich in ferns, mosses and lichens, as well as thistles, geraniums and foxgloves in season.

The area is well watered by *levadas.* You can follow paths to the Risco waterfall, or to the beauty spot known as the **Vinte e Cinco Fontes** (25 Springs), a pool into which scores of little water courses either drip or pour,

The unspoiled virgin vegetation of Rabaçal's hidden valley

the volume depending on the time of year and the amount of rainfall. (*See the* Risco Waterfall walk, *pp120–1.*)
65km northwest of Funchal, on the Paúl da Serra road to Porto Moniz.

Ribeira Brava

Ribeira Brava is a point along the island's southern coast where several roads and paths meet, so it started out as a watering hole where weary travellers would rest and refresh themselves before continuing on their journey.

Old habits die hard: even in these times of swift motorised transport, few Madeirans pass through the town without stopping for rest and a cup of coffee. This explains the unusually large seafront parking area, and the large number of nearby bars.

There is a small covered market, a miniature version of Funchal's Mercado dos Lavradores, where fish, flowers, fruit and vegetables are sold.

The name of the village, Ribeira Brava, means 'Wild River'. Most of the year you will search in vain for evidence that the river running to the west of the town deserves such a dramatic name, but heavy rains in autumn can see the water level rise 3–4m, and the bed is strewn with boulders and debris brought down from the mountains by flash floods.

The sea can be equally wild, hence the massive concrete breakwaters piled upon the pebble beach to absorb the force of the waves. You are unlikely to be tempted to swim here, but you may want to explore the little fishing harbour, to the east of the town, through an archway cut in the cliffs.

Gay sunshades add to the ambience at a pavement café, Ribeira Brava

In the grid of streets stretching north from the waterfront, you will find several characterful shops and typical examples of Madeiran town architecture – houses with ornate balconies and green window shutters.

Ribeira Brava is the start point for some attractive *levada* walks leading up the valley to the Boca da Encumeada pass. The town has two modern hotels that are popular with walkers.
32km west of Funchal.

São Bento (St Benedict)

On the main square, São Bento church is one of the most interesting on Madeira, with several features surviving from the original 16th-century building. One of these is the unusual painted stone font, carved with interlaced grapes,

Characterful Ribeira Brava

pomegranates, cable motifs and wild beasts, including wolves. Similar beasts are carved on the base of the wall pulpit and on the capitals of the arches nearest to the high altar. The original altar surround was moved to the left-hand aisle during modernisation work in 1948. It consists of a carved and gilded tabernacle and reredos with a Flemish painting of the Nativity above.

Much of the chancel, painted to resemble marble, is modern, but there is a 16th-century wooden sculpture of the Virgin above the high altar.

Ribeiro Frio

Most tour buses stop at Ribeiro Frio on the way to Santana, hence the size of the souvenir shop that dominates this little forest resort. The principal attraction is a trout farm, set in a pretty garden, with several concrete tanks fed by the fresh waters of the Ribeiro Frio (literally 'Cold River'), from which the place gets its name.

There is a limit to how long anyone can remain interested in the antics of thrashing rainbow trout, but if you have time to kill you can try exploring one of the nearby *levada* paths. These start just below the Ribeiro Frio's bar and restaurant, and are signposted. To the right is the path to Portela: for experienced walkers, this 12-km walk is well worth doing – it is considered one of the best walks on the island, but it does involve negotiating rock-cut tunnels and steep drops. Just about anybody could manage the first 15 minutes or so of the walk, however, which passes through an area of virgin laurel and heath woodland, typical of the vegetation which covered Madeira until clearance began in the 15th century.

A little further down the road from the bar is another signpost to the left labelled Balcões (meaning 'balconies'). After following this *levada* for 20 minutes you will reach the viewpoints to which the name refers, high above the valley of the Ribeira da Ametade. The panoramic views take in the high peaks of Madeira's central mountain range to the west, and the lumpy outline of Eagle Rock (Penha de Águia) on the northeast coast.
14km north of Funchal.

Santa Cruz

It is worth stopping at Santa Cruz even if the former tranquillity of this historic town has been sacrificed to the nearby airport and the busy 101 road. The church here, founded in 1533, is one of the least altered on the island, with its bulky bell tower, cross-shaped

Turning trout, Ribeiro Frio

One of Ribeiro Frio's *levada* paths

battlements and Gothic interior. Two other buildings of note nearby are the town hall and courthouse, and there is a colourful market on the seafront.
17km northeast of Funchal.

Santo da Serra

Santo da Serra occupies a low plateau to the east of Madeira. It has its own microclimate and is often under cloud, rain or mist when nearby Funchal is dry and sunny. Despite this, wealthy city merchants began to build mansions here from the 18th century and the area acquired a reputation as a healthy summer resort.

Today it is best known by sports-loving visitors as the location of a fine golf course (*see p157*) with sea views

from the fairways and pine plantations reminiscent of the Scottish Highlands. In the centre of the village is the entrance to an extensive public park (open daily during daylight hours) which locals know as the camellia garden because of the numerous camellias planted along the main central avenue. The extensive gardens, which once belonged to the Blandy family, also feature tennis courts, a children's playground and some sad-looking deer, ponies, birds of prey and a kangaroo kept within small enclosures. If you follow the main avenue downhill you will come to a viewpoint where you can look out to Ponta de São Lourenço and the easternmost tip of the island.
22km northeast of Funchal.

The courthouse in Santa Cruz

Santana

The lush valleys around Santana, the uncrowned capital of the north, are among the most beautiful and unspoiled on Madeira. In contrast with Funchal and the urbanised south of the island, Santana is undeveloped, a place where traditional Madeiran life continues unaffected by the modern world and where the intensively cultivated and terraced landscape is like a cross between Bali and the Alps.

Cutting and drying maize in Santana

You will have plenty of opportunity to observe the local agriculture as you journey to Santana, passing fields where cabbages, carrots, potatoes, yams and maize are grown, yielding two or even three crops a year. The roadsides and every patch of uncultivated land are ablaze with the crimson of red hot poker (known as 'fire flowers' in Portuguese), agave, poinsettia, fuchsia, nasturtiums or monbretia, depending on the time of year.

Thatched cowsheds (*see pp112–13*) dot the valley sides, and orchards provide apples, pears, plums, cherries, figs and mulberries. When you add to this the luscious blackberries, loganberries, strawberries and grapes, all grown locally, you will understand why the people of the region are nearly self-sufficient in food.

Santana is famous for its A-framed houses (*see pp112–13*). Right in the centre of the village is a house of this type open to visitors, inevitably part of a souvenir shop and restaurant complex, yet worth a look since it is authentically furnished and will give you an idea of how comfortable these houses can be.

You will see plenty of authentic examples as you wander along the village lanes, genuine lived-in houses set in impeccable gardens. These houses are often interspersed with tiny fields where barley and wheat are grown before being cropped by hand – partly for flour and animal feed, but also for thatching straw to keep the roofs repaired.

Santana is a good place to stop for lunch, since the main restaurant, the O Colmo, serves good locally produced food, including fresh trout from the farm at Ribeiro Frio (*see p106*) and delicious goat's cheese with honey.

Nearby

From Santana you can take the inland road southwards to **Queimadas**, the start point for several spectacular *levada* walks, including the one that goes to the well-named **Caldeirão do Inferno** (Hell's Cauldron). You can also continue to the end of the same road and walk up to the top of Madeira's highest peak, **Pico Ruivo** (*see p93*).

On the journey back from Santana, the view is dominated by the flat-topped **Penha de Águia** (Eagle Rock), which is a mountain-sized rocky outcrop which separates **Faial** and **Porto da Cruz**.

These two villages are typical of the little port towns that thrived in the era before motorised transport, when boats were used to carry goods around.

Porto da Cruz is a well-preserved example of a port town, with its ancient Roman-tiled houses and stone-built harbour. Few boats use it now, but the local children come here to dive and swim in the deep clean water, well sheltered from the powerful force of the Atlantic waves.

Porto da Cruz, once a bustling little port, now a peaceful and scenic backwater

Cowsheds and Palheiros

What is the difference between a cowshed and a traditional Madeiran *palheiros*, or A-framed house? You may ponder this question as you wander round Santana because in both cases the construction is identical: both have a triangular façade with a thatched roof sweeping from the gable ridge right down to the ground. One answer is that houses usually have pots of trailing geraniums by the door, and the façades are often boldly painted in crimson, white, yellow and blue. The other answer is, of course, that one has human occupants while the other is inhabited by a cow.

Cows in this part of Madeira cannot be left to roam – they would break their legs on the steep slopes, damage the terraces and destroy crops. For their own safety they are kept in a triangular byre: thatched roofs keep them warm in winter and cool in summer. They are milked daily and well looked after; you may see their owners climbing the hillside beneath a vast pile of grasses and hay with which they are fed. It is surprisingly roomy inside, like a *palheiros*, the human version.

The *palheiros* usually has an upper storey, reached by a ladder, for sleeping and storage. Separate toilets are placed

away from the house. Meals are prepared out of doors to avoid risk of fire, and prevent the cottage being filled with smoke and cooking smells.

Sometimes you will see sad examples of neglected cottages where the

Palheiros are colourful and surprisingly spacious, though their architecture differs little from the Maderian cowshed (below right)

owner has died or moved away. Without constant loving attention the houses soon decline, and the thatch is then replaced by ugly corrugated iron. So far, at least, this has not happened on a wide scale in Santana, and there are government incentive schemes which encourage the older people of Santana to maintain their traditional houses and lifestyle.

São Jorge

Fruit orchards and willow plantations dominate the scenic valleys between São Jorge and its neighbours, Arco de São Jorge and Boaventura. Tourist buses stop at the big As Cabanas shopping and restaurant complex just outside São Jorge. However, if you are not interested in embroidery and passion-fruit liqueurs you can visit the pretty Baroque church in the village, or take a refreshing stroll along the headland to the Ponta de São Jorge lighthouse, from where there are extensive views of the wild northern coastline.

Equally good are the views along the coast road to **Boaventura**. Here the main attraction is the peaceful cemetery set high up above the village church; romantic souls come here to visit the grave of Miss Turner, an American lady who died around 1925. Miss Turner was the owner of a thriving tearoom catering to English visitors in Santo da Serra, noted for its splendid garden. Her gardener would often talk about his home village of Boaventura, describing it as a paradise by the sea, beyond the Madeiran peaks. His descriptions fed

Playtime in Arco de São Jorge: building castles with discarded maize husks

her dreams and though she never visited the village, she requested that her mortal remains be buried in the Boaventura cemetery, a wish that was respected, even though it meant carrying her coffin over steep mountain tracks, since roads only came to the area in recent years. *50km north of Funchal.*

São Vicente

Most visitors to Madeira have to pass through São Vicente at some time because it is located at the junction of the island's spectacular north coast road and the main road to Ribeira Brava in the south. In an attempt to persuade travellers to stop and even stay a night or two, considerable sums have been spent on building new hotels and restaurants, and smartening the town up, so that it sparkles with an almost-too-pristine cleanliness, its buildings whitewashed to dazzling brightness.

The old town still has considerable charm, with its small, typically Madeiran general stores selling everything from pungent salt cod to religious statues. The simple parish church has colourful tiles and a painted ceiling. The modern church of **Nossa Senhora de Fátima**, with an eye-catching bell tower, and built between 1942 and 1953, stands high on a hill above the town. There is also a tiny chapel built in 1692 by the bridge at the mouth of the São Vicente River, which you will see if you head west to Porto Moniz on the north coast road.

Not to be missed is the **Grutas de São Vicente** (caves of Saint Vincent) at the Volcanism Centre, 1km up the valley from the Ribeira Brava – São Vicente road. The centre, surrounded by a lovely garden, provides visitors with audiovisual demonstrations of volcanic eruptions and explanations of how islands are formed. The underground caves are the result of an eruption over 400,000 years ago. They are a series of lava tubes measuring over 1,000m, of which 700m can be walked in about 30 minutes.

Multi-lingual tours are available hourly. The caves, at 40m underground and roughly a kilometre in length, are an easy walk. They were discovered in 1855 by an Englishman, James Johnson. It's doubtful that Johnson would recognise them now as the caves have been brought into the 21st century; for safety reasons they have been electrified, you can now stand up in them, and listen to piped-in music while you explore.

Still, with their dramatic rock pools and streams, and their café-au-lait coloured walls, the caves are one of Madeira's most popular and beautiful natural wonders.

Just before Porto Moniz, you will catch sight of the *janela* (window) in the offshore rocks, a feature which gives its name to the lush and scenic Ribeira da Janela ravine which cuts up to Rabaçal and Paúl da Serra.

If you have 4 hours to spare, take a rewarding walk up this valley, following the Levada da Central da Ribeira da Janela up from the car park and reservoir just above the village of Lamaceiros.

55km north of Funchal.

São Vicente's ancient chapel (top) and old town district (above) tempt travellers to stop

Madeira's roadside verges, *levada* paths and public parks are bright with flowers throughout the year. Thanks to the introduction of many South African plants which bloom in the depths of the northern hemisphere's winter, the botanical interest can be just as great in December as in August, and visitors arriving for Christmas festivities are greeted by rampant red agave flowers lining the airport road into Funchal. Some flowers bloom all year in Madeira's equable climate, including oleanders, red- and orange-flowered hibiscus and the aptly named Bird of Paradise (*Strelitzia reginae*) with its pointed, crest-like inflorescences. Winter-flowering plants include poinsettias, introduced from South America, with their scarlet leaves and gold stamens, camellias, orchids and arum lilies.

The many different varieties of mimosa that grow in the island's woods are also covered in powder-puff yellow flowers at this time of year. This woodland display is bettered only by the flowering of the jacaranda trees in central Funchal in April and May. Planted along all Funchal's main roads, their massed blossoms form a river of lilac blue when viewed from above –

descending from the hotel district, for example. Even as the jacaranda blossoms drop, the Pride of Bolivia (*Tipuana tipu*) picks up the baton, flowering in Avenida Zarco from June through much of the summer.

Summer is the season of massed agapanthus, which grow wild along

the waysides, of fragrant giant honey-suckles, of the even sweeter frangipani, and literally hundreds of other plants. Some will seem familiar, most of them wonderfully exotic.

If you want a basic illustrated guide, *The Plants and Flowers of Madeira* by António da Costa and Luis de O Franquinho is good value for money and widely available on the island.

Facing page above: Bougainvillaea can turn Funchal's rivers red; below: The tropical orchid, a native of South Africa
Above left: Golden Trumpet (*Atlamanda cathartica*) from South America; right: Indian fig tree and Mediterranean hibiscus
Left: South African Bird of Paradise (*Strelitzia*)

Drive: Western Madeira

This all-day tour of western Madeira will take you along the sunny southern coast, up to the contrasting moorlands of the Paúl da Serra, and down to Porto Moniz, returning along the spectacular north coast road and the Encumeada mountain pass.

The South Coast Road

Leaving Funchal on the EN101, you pass through the Estrada Monumental Hotel Zone and reach a picturesque fishing village, **Câmara de Lobos** (*see p79*) – going through a sea of banana plantations, which give way to grapevines on the higher slopes.

After another 7km you reach **Cabo Girão** (*see p75*). Those with a good head for heights can stop here to look down to the sea from the top of one of the world's highest cliffs (550m), marvelling at the tenacity of farmers who have cut little terraces into the face of the cliff.

After 11km, you get to **Ribeira Brava** (*see p105*): stop here for coffee, wander through the harbourside market, and visit São Bento, one of the island's oldest and most interesting churches.

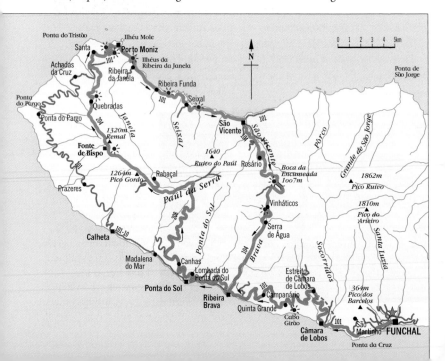

From here, ignore the right turn to São Vicente and carry on along the EN101 coastal road. After 3km the road divides: stay on the lower road which runs alongside the beach and through tunnels in steep cliffs dotted with tiny terraces.

Ponta do Sol (*see pp98–9*) is so called because it gets the sun all day, not being overshadowed by high mountains; hence you will see bananas grown everywhere, and packing stations where this economically important crop is processed for export.

Turn right, ignoring the EN101-10. After 3km you will reach **Canhas**, an important pilgrimage centre with a Via Sacra (Holy Way, or Stations of the Cross) running up through the village to a huge crucifix. Visit the place on the first Sunday in the month and you will encounter crowds of festive islanders at open-air mass. Next to the crucifix is an abandoned housing estate – islanders will give you different explanations for this ghost town – some say it was built by someone who won the national lottery, others that is was built by Venezuelan oil millionaires – in any event, the money ran out.

Paúl da Serra

Just west of Canhas you will meet the only dead straight stretch of road on Madeira. After 3km, turn right and drive 12km to the road junction at the top of the **Paúl da Serra plateau** (*see pp92–3*). Bear left on the EN204 towards Porto Moniz. After 5km you can divert right to Rabaçal for the Risco Waterfall walk (*see pp120–1*). The road across the bleak Paúl da Serra is raised above the moorland because of frequent flooding.

You will not see many other people, but you will see grazing sheep, goats and cows, and wind turbines which have been built to generate electricity.

Porto Moniz

Porto Moniz (*see pp100–1*) is reached after 25km. As you descend into this small north coast village, do not miss the viewpoint on the right from which you can look down on a pattern of tiny fields hedged with bracken. The village has several good fish restaurants.

Porto Moniz is the start point for a spectacular drive along the north coast, through Seixal to São Vicente. The 19-km road took 16 years to build and consists of tunnels cut through the cliffs, and ledges hacked out of the cliffside, offering intimate views of Atlantic breakers below – and cascading waterfalls above.

Boca da Encumeada

At São Vicente (*see pp114–15*) take the EN104 right, which climbs 12km up to the Encumeada Pass (*see p74*). Here a viewpoint allows you to look north and south down the two great ravines which almost split the island into two parts.

After a drive of 4km you pass one of the island's two *pousadas*, or government-owned inns, the Pousada dos Vinháticos (named after Madeira's native tree).

Just below is another viewpoint, from which you can look down on to a green and unspoiled valley, its sides sculpted into hundreds of tiny terraces.

After 10km you will return to Ribeira Brava. Then turn left, and simply retrace the morning's journey back to Funchal.

Walk: Risco Waterfall

Risco Waterfall is one of the most scenic spots on Madeira, and the short walk to the fall is well worth doing as a break from your tour of the west of the island.

Allow 30 minutes.

Rabaçal

To reach the start point of the walk, take the EN204, following the signs for Porto Moniz as you cross the empty moorland that characterises the Paúl da Serra plateau. Look for the sharp turning right that leads steeply downhill to Rabaçal.

Take great care along this road because it is only wide enough for one vehicle – use your horn at blind corners to warn other motorists of your presence. If you meet another vehicle, it is usual for the one climbing uphill to reverse to the nearest passing place. A short way down the road, you will drive across a river bed, albeit a very shallow one. This is the **Ribeira do Alecrim** (meaning 'Rosemary River'), named after the rosemary that grows along its pretty banks and pools.

After 2km you will come to a small car park, next to a government resthouse, which has picnic tables and a terrace. This is Rabaçal, a delightful spot: the name means 'virgin', 'primeval' or 'unspoiled', and looking out from the terrace over the green valley below it is not difficult to see why it has been given this name.

Levada do Risco

From the car park, follow the dirt track that leads downhill: it is on the right as you face the resthouse. Very soon this will bring you down to the **Levada do Risco**, which follows the valley side at a height of 1,030m.

The woodland on both sides of the *levada* is magical: the gnarled trees are hung with great hanks of lime green lichen, and wild goats feed among the many tumbled boulders that lie scattered across the hillside. The undergrowth consists of tree heath (*Erica arborea*).

The Levada do Risco passes under the **Risco Waterfall**, about a 30-minute walk from the car park. Although the area is beautiful it can be dangerous, that lovely green lichen that you were admiring at the beginning of the walk is wet and slippery the closer you get to the Risco Waterfall. As with other *levada* walks, wear walking shoes or boots with rubber soles for gripping. Pay attention to the warning signs along the trails and be careful not to continue beyond the waterfall, as the *levada* climbs higher it is wet, slippery and narrow.

Levada dos 25 Fontes

Following the path, you will pass a signposted junction – the way left leads downhill, and then right to the spot known as **Vinte e Cinco Fontes** (25 Springs). You can return later, if you wish, and take this path which leads, after about an hour, to a pool into which tumble numerous little waterfalls.

The route to Risco continues straight ahead, and as you pass along the path, sweeping views open up on the left, looking down the green and unspoiled valley of the Ribeira Grande.

Risco Waterfall

The sound of the waterfall will greet you before you see it. Just before the fall, the path divides: keep to the right, climbing up the concrete wall of the *levada* – and ignore the wider path to the left which leads a short way downhill to a reservoir and then stops. Rounding a corner, you will see the fall, its waters cascading from a height of 100m.

Don't be tempted to walk behind the fall; the ground and walls are extremely slippery and hazardous. If it is a warm day and you are overheated from the walk, simply relax and enjoy a close view of the fall while the mist soaks and cools you. You will dry off on the walk back to Rabaçal. For those accustomed to strenuous walks and climbs it will be tempting to continue on, but, again, heed the warning signs along the trail and do not walk beyond the fall.

The view from the Levada do Risco; high rainfall and humidity encourages the lush valley greenery and the growth of different types of lichen and moss

Drive: Central Madeira

If you have time for only one drive on Madeira, this is the one. It will take a whole day but is very varied, taking in burnt volcanic wastes, lush green valleys, wave-battered coasts and traditional island architecture and crafts.

To Monte

From Funchal, head north out of the city, following Rua 31 de Janeiro (that is, the right bank of the Ribeira de Santa Luzia). Follow the signs to Monte (*see pp88–9*): Monte is about 5km away. Having paid your respects to the former

Emperor Charles I of Austro-Hungary, entombed in the Monte church, and watched nervous passengers setting off on the Monte toboggan run, continue north on the EN103 for 3km to Terreiro da Luta, where you can see the statue of the Virgin Mary on a 5.5-m column, built as a World War I memorial.

Pico do Arieiro

After 3km, look for a byroad to the left which takes you through one of the island's national parks – if you miss the turning just go on to Poiso and turn left. Emerging from the park, turn left for 4km to reach Pico do Arieiro (*see p93*).

The landscape in the nature park and on the peak is volcanic. Little grows on the rusty red laterite soil, and a major reafforestation programme is under way. The forestry department faces an additional problem – the number of rabbits which nibble away at the vegetation, including recently planted tree seedlings. At the peak you can take a walk among the magnificent volcanic formations (*see p94*).

Ribeiro Frio

Backtrack to Poiso (the Abrigo do Poiso restaurant here is excellent, if you fancy lunch), then take the EN103 left to Ribeiro Frio (*see p106*), where you can watch the trout playing in the crystal clear waters of the local fish farm.

Heading on along the EN103, you will pass through Achada do Cedro Gordo – the name referring to the abundant crab apple trees grown for cider production – then through **Cruzinhas**, **Lombo de Cima**, **Degolada** and **Faial**.

This route takes you through gentle agricultural scenery, where the land is highly fertile and local farmers grow produce all year round, harvesting three, or even four, crops a year of beans, potatoes, carrots, cabbages or maize.

Santana

The landscape from Faial to Santana is dotted with colourful thatched traditional A-frame houses known as *paleiros*. Many of these are private homes, some are cowsheds; unless you step inside, it is hard to tell the difference between the two as all are well kept and beautiful. On an island such as Madeira, with high rocky slopes, cattle can easily fall off if they are left to graze freely, so they are kept in the cool shade of the *palheiros* and their owners bring them bales of fresh grass and hay several times a day. There are also several A-frame houses very near the centre of **Santana** (*see pp110–11*).

The village is fairly ordinary; there's a town hall, a small church and down on the hillside road there are several pretty squares. What makes it worth a night or two's stop is its location; just above a stunning cable car set along spectacular cliffs within view of glorious mountain scenery. Surrounding this is some of the most fertile farm land in Madeira, and grape vines, figs, kiwi, mulberries and plums grow in abundance here.

Continue driving to Faial heading along the EN101, the view is dominated by **Penha de Aguia** (Eagle Rock) rising to 590m. The lower portion of the rock is terraced fields, the upper half has been left forested, a perfect home for the ospreys that nest here seasonally. If you are inclined to climb Eagle Rock the footpaths to the summit are extremely rough; the climb takes about an hour and a half and is not recommended unless you are extremely fit.

Camacha

Taking the EN102 for 16km will bring you to Camacha, the centre of the island's wickerwork industry (*see pp80–1 & p147*). This is the best place to purchase souvenirs, and you can watch weavers creating beautiful crafts.

There is an easy *levada* walk nearby in the village of Vale Paraiso, 1.5km southwest of Camacha. The best way to reach it is by taxi; ask the driver to take you to the Levada da Serra Choupana. Once there it is a 90-minute walk on well marked trails through woodlands that open up to beautiful coastal scenery.

There is a Snack Bar along the trail that offers music and bottles of Murphy's for refreshment. Past the bar the *levada* reappears along a road, the Camino Municipal da Portela, follow the signs that read 'Camino da Portela Camacha'. This will take you on a steep downhill walk past the **Quinta Levada da Serra Hotel**, a few minutes after that take a sharp right and you are on the road to Camacha's church and main square. When it is time to return to Funchal from Camacha take the well travelled and signposted EN102 and EN101 roads.

Walk: Mountain Peaks

You can drive to the summit of Madeira's third highest peak, Pico do Arieiro (1,810m), in under an hour from central Funchal. Having arrived, the magnificent panoramas will tempt all but the most lethargic to take a walk.

The 3-hour walk from here to Madeira's highest peak, Pico Ruivo (1,862m), is rated one of the most spectacular on Madeira, but the going is very steep and recommended only to expert walkers, properly equipped. Non-experts can undertake the first 30 minutes of the walk, provided that the weather is good and that you have good non-slip walking shoes. You will also need a sweater and/or a windproof jacket in the winter months.

The mountain panorama seen from the Pico do Arieiro viewpoint

The walk begins to the left of the pousada *which is marked by a big yellow sign saying 'Pico Ruivo 10km'.*

Pico do Arieiro

You can spend the night on the summit of this mountain if you book in advance at the Pousada do Pico do Arieiro (*tel: (291) 230110*), the government-owned inn; the advantage is the opportunity to watch the sunset, gaze at the night sky away from the glare of city lights, and then observe the most spectacular dawn. Even if you do not make it here early enough for sunrise, you can get a taste of its colours at most times of the day because the sunlight, playing on the orange, purple, pink and brown volcanic rocks, makes their colours all the more intense.

To Viewpoint One

The first part of the walk follows a paved path, and the principal ingredients are silence (except for the wind) and spectacular views of deep cliffs and ravines on every side. The eerie silence continues as you approach the first *miradouro*, or viewpoint, and the sense of isolation is increased by the clouds that often cling to the valleys way beneath your feet, cutting you off from the sights and sounds of the noisy, busy world below. The view from the first *miradouro* is dominated by the long ridge of **Pico das Torres** (Peak of the Towers) to the north – so called because of the tower-like lumps and columns running up the jagged ridge to Madeira's second highest peak (1,851m).

To Viewpoint Two

The path now curls round, taking you to the western, and more sheltered, side of a cliff. A few disc-shaped house leeks growing out of the cinder-like rock cling to the cliff. Here you overlook the great gorge of **Ribeiro do Cidrão**. In the distance, ahead and to the left, is the great plateau of the Paúl da Serra rising above the clouds, marked by giant electricity-generating windmills with their huge propeller blades.

If you suffer from vertigo, this is probably as far as you should go. The 10-minute walk to the next viewpoint is very steep and at times the path is no more than a 2-m wide spine of rock, with sheer drops on either side – though there are iron railings and wire ropes to hold on to if you need help.

From the second *miradouro* you can see Pico Ruivo to the left, while Funchal, 22km away, may just be visible on a clear day. Turning round, far above you can see Pico do Arieiro, where you must now return. Don't worry, it is not such hard work as it looks; you should be back at the café on the peak for a well-earned drink within half an hour.

You can also see Pico do Arieiro from the saddle

what to see

Drive: Eastern Madeira

The eastern part of Madeira is the most developed, but it also has historic towns and dramatic seascapes. Although this tour can be done in half a day, take it at a more leisurely pace, perhaps stopping for a picnic or a swim.

Quinta do Palheiro Ferreiro

Leave Funchal on the EN101 east, after 3km turn left onto the EN102, signposted to Camacha. Turn right after 2km at the sign for 'Quinta do Palheiro'. Entering you will feel as if you have been transported to a pristine English garden (*see pp102–3*). The first owner, the wealthy Count Carvalhal, had a love affair with English landscapes, leading him to include woodland and grassy meadows when the estate was laid out in 1804. In 1885 John Blandy, an English wine merchant, purchased the estate and brought in plants from Japan, China and South Africa. It has been in the same family ever since.

Leaving the *quinta*, turn right, then first left, and then right again to rejoin the EN102. This will take you to Camacha (*see p78*).

Santo da Serra

Continue along the EN102 for another 11km and you will reach Santo da Serra (*see p108*) with its miniature zoo and extensive park, known locally as the camellia garden – though plenty of other plants grow here as well. The road from Santo da Serra is dotted with

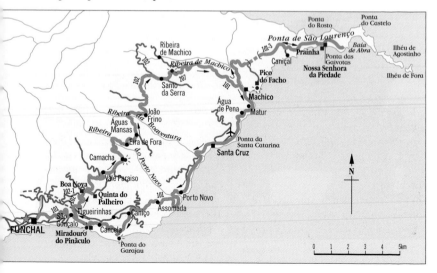

holiday villas. Turn left after 1.6km, then right after 2.2km, rejoining the EN101 eastwards, signposted to Machico. After 6km, before reaching Machico, turn left on the EN101-3 signposted to Caniçal and the Zona Franca Industrial.

The road passes through a tunnel, then skirts Caniçal, heading for Ponta de São Lourenço: just east of Caniçal is a new industrial estate, a blot on the landscape, but designed to keep industry out of built-up residential districts. The industrial estate occupies the site of the island's now-redundant whale processing factory (*see p130*).

The sun setting over Ponta de São Lourenço

Ponta de São Lourenço

Soon you will pass the artificial landscape of the industrial zone, and return to volcanic rocks in various shades of orange and brown. A sign to the right, after 1.5km, points to Prainha, the location of the island's only naturally sandy beach, a place for swimming in the turquoise-coloured seas.

At the end of the road, you can walk out along the rugged headland of Ponta de São Lourenço (*see pp128–9*) for wonderful views. In the car park, two old men sell trinkets made from discarded whalebone. To learn more about this now defunct industry, you can visit the whaling museum in Caniçal (*see p82*), where you can also watch tuna fishermen mending their boats or bringing in the catch.

Machico

A short drive back along the EN101-3 will bring you to Machico (*see pp86–7*), the ancient capital of the eastern part of the island, now a buzzing resort town. Worth visiting is the Manueline-style

parish church and the peaceful cemetery just downhill from the Dom Pedro Baía hotel, a spot colonised by some of the island's most spectacular flowers.

Santa Cruz

The road from Machico to Santa Cruz passes under the airport runway – the runway is built on huge concrete pillars, and if a plane is coming in, it may seem as if it is about to land on your car roof!

In Santa Cruz (*see pp107–8*), the tower of the 16th-century parish church beckons; it is joined on the same square by the equally ancient Câmara Municipal, or Town Hall.

Caniço

The last stop before you return to Funchal, Caniço (*see pp82–3*) looks like a developed resort village, but you should continue down to the coast at **Ponta do Garajau**, not so much for the outsize statue of Christ as for the beach area with its views, its coloured rocks and the stands of prickly pear cactus. From the beach, turn left at the first junction to rejoin the EN101 Funchal road at Cancela.

Walk: Ponta de São Lourenço

This 3-hour walk is rigorous but it provides some breathing space on your tour of eastern Madeira. A good place to stop off and stretch your legs exploring the massive cliffs and bays at the tip of the island, enjoying lovely views of the coast and the wind turbines.

Developments around Caniçal to create the industrial free port have tamed the landscape as you approach the island's easternmost point, but you will then pass through a lunar landscape of burnt orange and chocolate brown soils as you

Modern wind turbines contrast with the primeval ruggedness of the volcanic landscape at the island's eastern tip

approach the end of the tarmac road. Leave the car here and climb the rocks to the right of the car park, to a picnic area with tables and chairs – and a panoramic view of the Baia de Abra, and the Ilhas Desertas (Deserted Isles) in the distance.

The Walk

Two rusty iron posts by the car park mark the beginning of the walk. Shortly after, the track divides. You should ignore the wide track that leads upwards and straight ahead; instead, bear right and downhill to the bottom of a shallow valley, then up the other side, keeping the wide view of the bay to your right.

As you climb the ridge ahead, the views become more and more dramatic, and the sunshine heightens the vivid colours of the striped cliff-faces on your right, resembling a section through a giant layer cake.

Flora

The dry thin soil of this headland supports a different mix of plants to other parts of the island, including some noble members of the often-maligned thistle family. You may see *Silybum marianum*, the milk thistle, which has bold white-veined leaves and striking flowers. Another very prickly specimen is the horned, or Mexican, poppy (*Argemone mexicana*), with its big papery yellow flowers and bright orange sap. The most abundant of the thistles here is the prickly cardoon (*Eynara cardunculus*), a relative of the artichoke, with big, sweetly scented flowers, much visited by bees and other insects.

Views

After 20 minutes of strenuous uphill climbing, you will reach a drystone wall built of boulders, with a gap for walkers to pass through. Beyond this point there are scores of tracks eroded by sheep and visitors – bear leftwards, descending gradually across the bare biscuit-coloured bedrock. Before long you will reach a flat area, with views to the left down a rock ravine. Down below, Atlantic waves dash against the raw red cliffs of the island's north face.

If you like you can take a path to the left that gives access to an even more breathtaking view, but only for those with a head for heights. From here on the path is more easy to follow. It leads eastwards to a ridge on which sits a telegraph pole – you are not aiming for the pole itself, but the rock platform higher up to the left of it.

Here you can sit and admire views that stretch far in every direction. To the east you can see the lighthouse on the tip of **Ilhéu de Fora**, the island at the easternmost tip of Madeira. Further to the right is an eyelet or window in the rocky headland called **Ponta do Furado**, and beyond that, the flat-topped Ilhas Desertas are normally visible (if not, local lore says it will soon rain).

This is a very different Madeira from the green, flower-filled interior of the island; bleak and inhospitable but none the less beautiful. Here you can enjoy real solitude, alone with the buzzards, hawks and other birds of prey that you may see wheeling overhead as you return to the car park at the start of the walk.

Whaling and Conservation

Visitors to Ponta de São Lourenço will see old men selling trinkets made of whalebone ivory, the last sad remnants of an industry that is no more, for the hunting and killing of whales finally stopped in Madeiran waters in June 1981. The proposal to turn the waters of the archipelago into a marine reserve for ocean mammals is still to take off for the protection of not just sperm whales, but also the dolphins that are still hunted for their meat and the monk seals that are persecuted because they are perceived as competing with Madeira's fishermen for commercial fish stocks.

If the scheme is realised, the sight of sperm whales playing in the waters off Madeira may once again become relatively common. That, at least, is the hope of marine biologists working for the Society for the Protection of Sea Mammals who have been conducting research into whale migration in Madeiran waters since 1985.

It is heartening to report that the researchers are being greatly aided by former whaling fishermen, who are now using their knowledge and experience of the sperm whales' habits to help protect the very same creatures that they used to hunt.

Ponta de São Lourenço (facing page); relics of an extinct industry – scrimshaw and boats carved from whale ivory (below)

Getting Away From It All

*'God created the world and was so pleased
with His work that He gave it a kiss and
Madeira was born.'*

MADEIRAN MYTH

Waters around Madeira
teem with fish

Boat Trips

Madeira is rich territory for those who
want to get away from it all; an island of
wild places and endless meandering
footpaths (*see p136*). Another way to
escape is to head for the sea; by joining
a mini cruise you can see the island's
towering cliffs from a different
perspective, and returning to Funchal
harbour you will retrace the sea route
taken by all visitors to Madeira in the
past, before the first commercial
aeroplane services began in 1964.

The Wind and the Sea

The best half-day excursions by boat
take you along the island's southern
coast, either eastwards to **Baia de Abra**,
or westwards to **Ponta do Sol**, passing
the foot of **Cabo Girão**, one of the
world's highest sea cliffs. Some operators
anchor off the island for a while so that
you can swim: the waters are very clean
and the sea temperature rarely falls
below 18°C even in December and
January. Evening excursions are timed
to make the most of the sunset.

Most operators use motorboats, but
you can also spend a day at sea under
sail on the 20-m yacht *Albatroz*, built in
1939 and beautifully restored. All boat
excursions depart from Funchal's yacht
marina, and you can book either direct
at the marina offices or through travel
agents.

The Ilhas Desertas

For the ultimate away-from-it-all
experience you can join one of the
occasional boat trips that go to the Ilhas
Desertas, the three flat islands 20km to
the southeast of Funchal. The largest of
the islands, **Deserta Grande**, is a long,
narrow, 12km-by-1km plateau of
volcanic rock rising to a height of 479m.

The island is arid and the soil is too
thin to support crops, though it is home
to the very rare, big wolf spider (*Lycosa
ingens*), which is black, ferocious and so
poisonous that its bite can cause death
to humans. All attempts to inhabit
Deserta Grande have been shortlived.

However, there is a biological
observatory on the island manned by
naturalists. Their job is to monitor and
protect the wildlife, notably a small
colony of monk seals. The seals were
once numerous, but raids by Madeiran
fishermen resulted in mass slaughter
and their near extinction: the fishermen
regarded the fish-eating seals as a threat
to their livelihood.

The fishermen also killed half the
island's bird population in another raid
in 1976. To prevent further bloodshed,
the island was declared a nature reserve

in 1990. Visitors can visit the island only with a special permit granted exclusively to people engaged in legitimate research projects. You can, however, sail to the islands to watch the seals, and you may also catch sight of dolphins and turtles.

There are also many sea birds to be seen around the islands, including Cory's, Manx and the Madeiran little shearwater, plus Bulwer's soft-plumaged and Madeiran petrels. A visit to Funchal's Municipal Museum (*see p50*) will help you identify all of these.

Gaviao, based in Funchal's marina, runs boat trips to the **Ilhas Desertas** every Thursday (weather permitting) departing at 10am and returning at 6.30pm, *tel: (291) 241124* for details. Only one company, the **Porto Santo Line** (*tel: (291) 210317*), offers trips ashore on Wednesdays and Saturdays.

Sport Fishing
Big fish abound in the deep waters off Madeira, and regular excursions depart from Funchal's marina in search of marlin, tuna, swordfish and shark. If you

happen to be passing the marina when the fishing boats come in, you can watch the proud anglers posing for a photograph with their catch alongside a chalk board that records the length and weight of the prize.

Trips can be arranged through travel agents or through Capt. Ron Cowling at Madeira Big Game Fishing (tel: (291) 231823); www.madeiragamefish.com

Undersea Exploration
For those who prefer to watch and admire the strange creatures of the deep rather than hunt them, there are several diving centres on Madeira and Porto Santo.

Scorpio Divers (*Complexo do Lido, Funchal, tel: (291) 746977*) takes on everyone, from absolute beginners to experienced divers, and is a British-run sub-aqua club with certified instructors, based in Funchal's Hotel Zone.

Atalaia, based in Caniço, offers equipment hire and courses (tel: (291) 934330). So does Urs Moser Diving School (tel: (291) 982162) on Porto Santo (see pp140–1), though only from May to October.

A boat trip will give you a different perspective on Madeira's dramatic scenery

If you have never been diving before in your life, Madeira is the place to have a go, with several schools catering for absolute beginners (*see p133*). The clear blue seas round Madeira's southern coast are rich in underwater caves where you can marvel at the variety of the vegetation and the agility of the multi-coloured fish.

that cling to the black basalt rocks of the sea bed, the coral-coloured scorpion fish, and the teeming shoals of tiny fish whose iridescent stripes flash in the gloom as they twist and turn. Parrot fish, named for the parrot-beak shape of their mouths, may come up to investigate you: the bright red fish are female, the dull blue are male.

Some 4km out from the shore you may encounter hammerhead sharks, big-eye tuna and barracuda, the kind of big fish that excite sporting anglers and the island's commercial fishermen, but inshore you are not likely to encounter anything more ferocious than a moray eel.

Sea bream, mullet and sea perch are quite common, as are squid and octopus, but the real gems of the underwater world are the sea anemone

All is not so perfect, however, in this undersea world, and diving round Madeira will also bring home just how dirty humans are – rubbish mars the sea bed, just as it does the island's footpaths.

Conscious of this, the Madeiran authorities have declared parts of the coast a marine nature reserve, out of bounds to fishermen, backed by regular coastal patrols and efforts to clean up the pollution.

The sea around the island is rich with the variety of plant and animal marine life, such as parrot fish (facing page); commercial fisherman (above).

Hiking

There were very few roads on Madeira until the 1960s – instead, a complex network of footpaths crisscrossed the island, linking up with the equally extensive system of pathways running alongside the island's *levadas*, or irrigation canals (*see pp138–9*). These footpaths make Madeira a wonderful place for long-distance walking, with all the attractions of panoramic views, waterfalls, scented woodlands, abundant flora and arresting geological formations. A good map is essential.

Beginners

Although Madeira's climate is balmy – it can get rather warm when walking the uphill and downhill footpaths – be sure to wear light clothing, absorbent socks and sturdy boots. Four walks along well-trodden footpaths are detailed in this guide (*see pp70–1, pp120–1, pp124–5, & pp128–9*). To get the most pleasure out of *levada* walking you might consider joining guided walks. Walks with specialists such as **Strawberry World** (Lido Tours) (*Centro Comercial Monumental Lido, Estrada Monumental, Funchal, tel: (291) 762429*) are led by knowledgeable mountain guides. Tours can be booked directly with the company, or through travel agents or the tourist office in Funchal.

Footwear and Clothing

Not all of Madeira is easy for walking; there are many treacherous mountain paths, particularly with the *levadas*. It is important to bring the proper footwear; you will need mountain boots, particularly for walking/hiking the

Well worth the effort: the view from Balcões

levadas. They should be waterproof and have a good grip to prevent slipping on wet rocks, mossy paths and scree slopes. Also bring lightweight clothing, sun block, a waterproof windbreaker and a hat. Every year many unprepared visitors suffer serious injuries, some requiring hospitalisation, because they trip or slip walking the mountainous regions of Madeira.

Experienced Walkers

The bible for serious walkers on Madeira is John and Pat Underwood's *Landscapes of Madeira*, which is sold in just about every newsagents and souvenir shop on the island. Opinions differ, naturally enough, on which walks are the very best, but if you are short of time, most people agree that the following three are difficult to beat for variety and scenic value:

• Pico do Arieiro to Pico Ruivo (*the first part of this route is covered on p124*)

• Rabaçal to the waterfall at Risco and Vinte e Cinco Fontes (*part covered on p120*)
• Queimadas to the Caldeirão do Inferno (Hell's Cauldron, *see p110*).

Planning and Precautions
Nothing in the world is ever perfect, and the big drawback for walkers on Madeira is the cost and time involved in getting to and from the start and end points of your walk. Some people get round this by camping or sleeping out under the stars, but by adopting this approach you miss one of Madeira's big attractions: the chance to walk all day among mountain peaks and then retire at night not to some sweaty alpine hut, but to a comfortable hotel with a shower and a good restaurant.

Buses offer a cheap and reliable way of getting to and from your walk, but for optimum freedom it is best to hire a car or use a taxi. If you team up with other walkers you can share the cost between four or five – it is, in any case, advisable not to go walking on your own in case you have an accident.

If you do go out alone, be sure to tell someone where you are going and what time you can be expected back so that the alarm can be raised if you fail to return.

Many beautiful parts of the island are accessible only on foot

The *levadas* of Madeira are a unique and endearing feature of the island, forming an astonishing network of irrigation canals, some 2,150km in total length. The earliest canals date right back to the colonisation of the island in the 15th and 16th centuries, though most were dug, entirely by hand, in the early part of the 20th century.

The purpose of *levadas* is to distribute water from those parts of the island that have plenty – notably the north side, where average annual rainfall tops 2m – to the dry areas, such as the sunny south where the economically important grape and banana crops are grown.

The *levadas* are fed both by natural springs and by reservoirs – giant storage tanks built up in the mountains. Water from the outfalls is first put to work driving the turbines of the island's electricity-generating power stations.

Maintaining the *levadas* is an important job, entrusted to the *levadeiro*, who patrols his allotted length of *levada* to keep the waters flowing, clear up landslips and unblock grilles designed to filter out leaves and debris. He is also responsible for operating the complex system of sluices and watergates which divert water to the individual properties bordering the *levada* according to a carefully worked out schedule.

To do this, the *levadeiro* needs access to the water channels – hence the footpaths that run alongside, built for purely functional reasons but

Levadas penetrate where no roads go, and the *levadeiro* (left) maintains his stretch of canal

coincidentally offering a paradise for walkers. They penetrate the most inaccessible depths of the island, running up the sides of deep ravines and carefully terraced valleys, always following the contours of the terrain so that, once you are on the path, there is no strenuous climbing.

The path they weave is always varied, sometimes passing through rock-cut tunnels, at other times through ancient woodland hung with moss and lichens, and sometimes alongside sunny cherry orchards or market gardens. Best of all, they take you to places where the modern world has yet to penetrate, far from the sound of traffic, but full of the sounds of birds and gently running water.

Porto Santo

If sun, sea and sand are what you are looking for, then you probably will not have chosen Madeira for your holiday. Porto Santo, on the other hand, has all three and not much else. Porto Santo's 9-km long sandy beach runs almost the entire length of the island's southern coast. Anywhere else this beach would now be backed by scores of high-rise hotels, but sheer remoteness has ensured that Porto Santo's beach remains undeveloped and unspoilt, a paradise for those who enjoy idle sunbathing or more active water sports, such as windsurfing.

Getting There

There are several flights a day between Santa Catarina airport and Porto Santo. The 37-km journey takes a mere 15 minutes. The fare price is quite high but

Remoteness guarantees unspoilt beaches

flights are often fully booked in the summer season, so it is advisable to book in advance through TAP (Air Portugal), *Avenida das Comunidades Madeirenses 10* (*tel: (291) 239211*) or through a travel agent.

By sea, the journey is on a luxury cruise liner equipped with cinemas, restaurants and game rooms, it takes two and a half hours depending on the weather. If the sea is rough people prone to seasickness should consider flying. Ships leave Funchal's marina at 8am and return by 10pm. Bookings can be made through any travel agent or direct with the cruise line office on the marina, Porto Santo Line (*tel: (291) 210 300*). There is a car ferry that sails daily from Funchal, but the journey takes about 5 hours.

Getting Around

It is a 20-minute walk or a very short taxi ride from the ferry port or airport to the beach and to **Vila Baleira**, Porto Santo's only town. If you want to tour

Porto Santo's seemingly endless ribbon of sand

the island, taxis can be hired at the ports or in Vila Baleira. Alternatively, you can rent a car, book a boat trip around the island or join a guided tour; just head for the seafront shops in Vila Baleira and you will find all these options on offer.

For the more adventurous, the Urs Moser Diving Centre hires out bicycles and motorcycles, and also organises diving and boat trips; they are situated at *Rua João Gonçalves 5, Vila Baleira* (*tel: (291) 982162*).

The Island's Character
Porto Santo is a pretty uncomplicated place for most of the year – it gets crowded only in August when Madeirans flock over for their annual holiday. The airport, which serves as a reserve NATO airbase, saw action during the Falklands campaign and the Gulf War, but for most of the time the islanders enjoy a peaceful existence, tending tiny plots where figs, melons, grapes and pumpkins are grown.

Windmills dot the hill tops, built to generate electricity, although there is at least one ancient structure with canvas sails which is still grinding corn in the traditional manner. Donkeys are used for transport, and the upland areas are grazed by cattle and sheep.

Overall, the island looks brown and arid, but there are springs on the island feeding the irrigation system, and one of them produces bottled mineral water.

Porto Santo

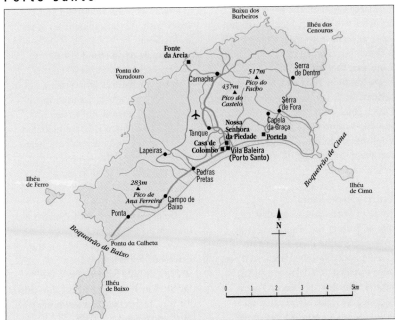

History

Apart from the fact that **Porto Santo** was the first island to be 'discovered' by Zarco in 1418 (*see p10*), it is more famous for someone else: Christopher Columbus.

Columbus married the daughter of the island's first governor (*see p15*) and he reportedly lived on Porto Santo at the Casa de Colombo (House of Columbus) at *Rua Cristovao Colombo 12 (open: Tue–Fri 10am–6pm & Sat–Sun 10am–1pm. Free admission)*. The museum has been restored and is made up of a number of rooms of artifacts connected with Columbus and the island's history. There are portraits of Columbus with scenes depicting some of his many adventures. You can view maps of his journeys and models of several of his boats.

A large room off the courtyard contains two sunken grain stores and treasures recovered from the *Carrock*, a Dutch boat owned by the East India Company that sank off the coast of Porto Santo in 1724 while on route to Jakarta. In the museum are Spanish and Dutch coins and silver ingots. Most of the ship's cargo was salvaged by an Englishman, John Letbridge in 1726, the rest was recovered in 1974 and donated to the museum.

Touring Porto Santo

Tours of Porto Santo normally take in one or both of the island's volcanic cones; one is the **Pico do Castelo** (Castle Peak), so called because it was once fortified as a defence against pirates; the other is **Pico do Facho** (Torch Peak), the island's highest point (517m), where sentries once

Volcanic peaks tower over Porto Santo's yachting marina

lit warning beacons if pirates were sighted. There are wonderful views from both hill tops, sometimes as far as Madeira.

Fonte da Areia (Sand Spring) is where the island's mineral water is bottled, the natural spring rising out of the sandstone which has been much eroded by the wind and waves.

Serra de Dentro is an uninhabited village, picturesque in its decay, where sheep now graze the vegetation that cloaks the abandoned terraces.

Staying On

If you are hooked on Porto Santo's lazy lifestyle, or want to put in some serious sun worship, the place to stay is the luxurious Porto Santo Hotel (*tel: (291) 982381*) in Vila Baleira where the facilities include windsurfing equipment for hire, tennis courts, a swimming pool and a good restaurant.

There are any number of viewpoints that offer awe-inspiring vistas of natural beauty

Shopping

Part of the pleasure of shopping in Madeira is watching souvenirs being made before you buy them. Factories producing embroidery or wickerwork put on demonstrations, and they don't make you feel obliged to buy anything. In fact, Madeiran shopkeepers do not go in for high-pressure sales techniques at all and the welcome absence of hassle only adds to the pleasure of browsing through Funchal's many shops.

Portuguese leatherwork is renowned for quality and is keenly priced

The best shops are located in the streets immediately north and south of the cathedral. If you are exploring this area, don't forget to look down the little side alleys, as well as the main streets, where some of the most characterful shops are tucked away.

Practical Details

Madeira is a shoppers' and bargain hunters' paradise. There are plenty of shopping centres located in Funchal, and the good part is that they are open from 10am–10pm daily (except Sundays in some towns). Funchal's most established shopping streets are near the marina and the Avenida Arriaga to Avenida Zarco and up to Rua Fernao Ornelas and any avenue in between. Take a city map and go exploring to find that something special to take home. Don't just shop the main avenues, the narrow back streets have some interesting shops also. There are many shops offering the two most popular souvenir items: wicker and embroidery.

If you crave a mall atmosphere then head to Madeira Shopping, the largest shopping centre on the island, in the Santa Quiteria section of Funchal. Here you will find, under one roof, 83 shops, 7 cinemas, 20 restaurants (some with terraces offering a view of the sea) and what Madeirans call Microlandia – bowling, virtual reality machines and mini golf.

What to Buy and Where
Antiques

Furniture, mirrors, copper pans, old *azulejos* tiles, or even handcarved crib figures – all these are worth looking out for in the little cluster of antique shops that you will find opposite São Pedro church.

Bolo do Mel

If you get hooked on Madeira's solid and filling honey cake you can buy supplies to take home at numerous *pastelaria*, or baker's shops, such as the one at *Rua da Carreira 75*. The cake will keep for many months but traditionally a new batch is made on 8 December ready for the Christmas festivities, and any old cake is eaten up on the same day.

Books

If you run out of books to read by the hotel pool, you can buy all the latest English bestsellers at the **Patio Bookshop**, Rua da Carreira 43. The shop also sells guidebooks and usually has a small stock of very interesting illustrated antiquarian guides to Madeira; these make an unusual souvenir and bring back a sense of the island's recent British 'colonial' past.

Boots

You can buy traditional Madeiran leather boots with a turned-down top at roadside stalls and souvenir shops all over Madeira. If you want to see how they are made, visit **Gonçalves & Silva**'s workshop at *Rua do Portão de São Tiago 22*, in the Zona Velha (Old Town).

Embroidery

Handmade embroidery (*bordados*) is one of the island's most important exports (*see pp148–9*), and there is a huge choice of shops all over Funchal stocking the genuine product, as well as cheap machine-made imitations.

Genuine handmade embroidery always carries a lead tag fixed to one corner as a guarantee of quality awarded by the island's handicraft institute,

IBTAM (*see p38*). In any case, you will soon learn to recognise the genuine article, which is very elegant but also rather expensive, being a labour-intensive product.

Some of the big exporters welcome visitors to their factory showrooms where you can watch the pattern printing processes and the final finishing of garments and table linen. One of the best is **Patricio & Gouveia**, at *Rua do Visconde de Anadia 33*. The biggest choice is to be found, appropriately enough, in Rua dos Murcas (Mercers' Street), where every other shop sells embroidery.

Exquisitely embroidered, but beware of imported machine-made copies

Flowers

Shopping for flowers in the Mercado dos Lavradores, or Workers' Market (*see p44*), can be great fun but, if you want your flowers packed in special boxes for travelling it is best to buy from a florist. **A Rosa** at *Rua Imperatriz D Amélia 126 (behind the Savoy Hotel in the Hotel Zone)*, will pack and deliver freshly-cut flowers to your hotel if you order them two or three days before departure, and most tour operators can organise this at no extra charge.

Popular, long-lasting Madeiran flowers include orchids (in season from late November to May), *strelitzias* (birds of paradise) and anthuriums (flamingo flowers), the last two available all year. You can also take home bulbs, seeds and baby orchid plants, provided that there is no soil with them.

Food

Gourmets will enjoy browsing in little delicatessens such as the one at *Rua do Carmo 11*. Best buys are Portuguese olive oil, fresh walnuts in season and *lapas escabeche*, limpets preserved in brine and vinegar, an unusual ingredient for a seafood salad or pasta sauce.

Hats

Bobble hats with earflaps, as worn by Madeiran farmers to keep off the rain, or straw boaters, as worn by Monte toboggan drivers, can always be bought from roadside stalls – or try **Salão Londrino**, *Rua dos Ferreiros 128*.

Leather

Shoes, bags, belts and clothing, mostly imported from the Portuguese

Cottons come in all colours and designs

mainland, are very good value if you compare prices here with the fashion shops of northern Europe. To see a good range of stock visit **Pele**, *Rua dos Murcas 26*, or **Arte Couro**, *Rua da Alfândega 15*.

For really upmarket but still affordable products, the best stockists are: **Charles**, *Largo do Chafariz 22*; **Yaya**, *Rua Câmara Pestana 3*; **Godiva**, *Avenida Arriaga 11–13*; **Chloé**, *Largo do Phelps 12*.

Knitwear

Knitted cotton sweaters and cardigans are another bargain. They are bought at wayside stalls by visitors who discover how much colder it can be in Madeira's mountains. In Funchal, you will see a good selection at *Rua dos Murcas 4*.

Pottery, Porcelain, Glass and Home Furnishings

Casa Turistica, in *Rua do Conselheiro José Silvestre Ribeiro*, is a must for all kinds of souvenirs, but especially for ceramics – whether you want just a cachepot for your potted plants or a full dinner service. The shop is laid out like a cross between a private mansion and a museum, with antiques and oil paintings hung beneath ornate plastered ceilings and forming a background for excellent displays.

Other good stores selling contemporary Portuguese designs in textile, pottery, furniture or glass include **Cayres**, *Rua Dr Fernão Ornelas 56* and **Galeria das Louças**, in *Rua do Sabão*.

Souvenirs

Among the less expensive are dolls in Madeiran costume, musical instruments such as the percussive *brinquinho*, videotapes of the island and miniature bottles of island liqueurs. **Madeira Sun**, *Avenida Zarco 4*, sells all the typical souvenirs, as does the **Bazar Monte Carlo**, *Rua dos Murcas 19* and **Rosa d'Ouro**, *Rua de António José d'Almeida*.

Tapestry

The craft of sewing pictures on canvas was introduced to Madeira by the German artist, Herbert Kiekeben, in 1938. The **Kiekeben** shop, at *Rua da Carreira 194*, sells wallhangings, chair covers, handbags and carpets, and you can buy do-it-yourself tapestry kits in **Madeira Sun**, *Avenida Zarco 4*.

Wickerwork

The heart of wicker production is at Camacha (*see p78 & pp80–1*), and although some wickerwork may be purchased throughout the island it is to this village that the visitor should head for the complete range of products and for demonstrations by craftsmen at work. However, if Camacha is not on your itinerary, there is a well-stocked shop in Funchal, at *Rua da Carreira 102*.

Wines and Liqueurs

Many Madeiran souvenir shops sell miniatures and full bottles of non-vintage Madeira, but serious wine lovers should visit Funchal's various wine lodges. The best known is the **Adegas de São Francisco** (*see p30*) which has a tasting bar and a well-stocked shop, but you should also visit **D'Oliveiras**, at *Rua dos Ferreiros 107*, an old wine lodge full of dark timbers and delicious smells, or its near neighbour, **Henriques & Henriques**, at *Rua dos Ferreiros 125*, whose central courtyard is shaded by rampant vines.

Madeira Shopping

A complete contrast is to be found in Madeira's largest shopping centre, where you will find more than 100 shops that sell designer clothes and electrical goods, an English cinema, and most, if not all, of the famous American fast-food outlets.

Long-lasting Madeiran cut flowers

Embroidery

1,000 women employed in the business.

Today, that number has grown to 20,000 embroiderers, but this remains a cottage-based industry. Whole families, including men and boys, are

The art of embroidery was introduced to Madeira by Elizabeth Phelps, daughter of a British wine shipper, during the 1850s, a time of particular calamity on Madeira: cholera struck the island in 1852, carrying off 7,000 victims, and disease devastated the vine crops later in the same year. The resulting poverty so distressed Miss Phelps that she established her embroidery business as a means of supplementing the islanders' meagre incomes. The samples Miss Phelps took to London were warmly received, and by 1862 there were

involved, and the embroiderers love to tell the cautionary tale of a husband and wife team who together worked a huge tablecloth, starting at opposite ends. Only when the work was well advanced did they discover that the husband was sewing one face of the cloth, his wife the other!

You can understand how easily this might happen if you visit one of the island's several embroidery 'factories' where the designs are pricked out on to the linen before it is sent to outworkers, and where, once the embroiderers have finished their work, the cloth is finished, washed, ironed and then given the special IBTAM seal.

This metal tag, found on all genuine Madeiran embroidery, is a guarantee of authenticity granted by the island's handicrafts institute (*see p38*). It also guarantees a high price, since Madeiran embroidery is far from cheap, but you will understand why once you have seen the quality of the work and the beauty of the intricate floral designs.

Thousands of hours of meticulous work go into the design, production and finishing of Madeiran embroidery

Entertainment

For the older crowd, entertainment on Madeira revolves principally around its many five-star hotels, such as the **Hotel Classic Savoy**, the **Pestana Carlton Park Resort & Casino Funchal** and the **Pestana Carlton Madeira**. Their shows, casinos and folklore evenings are widely advertised. They are open to everyone.

Roulette at the Casino

Shows

The Hotel Classic Savoy

The Savoy's regular *This Is Madeira* show is one of the liveliest shows in the hotel loop. Local performers give a musical history of many of the island's traditional songs and dances (*see pp152–3*), they mingle with the audience explaining their costumes and instruments. Tea dances and jazz nights are also featured on the hotel's entertainment schedule.
Avenida do Infante. Tel: (291) 775936.

Pestana Carlton Madeira

The Monday night programme in the Atlantico dining room features the folklore and dance customs of Madeira. Thursdays there's a string quartet playing the classical music of Strauss, Vivaldi and Mozart. Saturdays a French-style cabaret is the headline programme.
Largo Antonio Nobre. Tel: (291) 239500.

Pestana Carlton Park Resort & Casino Funchal

The Pestana Carlton Park Resort & Casino offers four shows a week that feature songs and routines from popular Broadway musicals. There's also an Oldies show with hits of the 1960s up to the present and, on Sundays, a Paris review featuring the cancan.

Prices include a four-course dinner, as well as free entrance after the shows to the casino and the Copa Cabana disco.
Rua Imperatriz Dona Amelia.
Tel: (291) 209100.

Casino

The Madeira Casino

Located in the grounds of the Carlton Park Hotel, the Casino da Madeira offers visitors the opportunity to throw away large sums of money playing roulette, blackjack or the slot machines.

The Casino is open from 5pm to 3am Sunday–Thursday for people over 21 years of age. You must show your passport to gain entry, and men are expected to wear a jacket and tie.
Carlton Park Hotel. Tel: (291) 209100.

Cinema

Popular blockbuster films are shown in the original language (usually English), with Portuguese subtitles at several cinemas in Funchal – their schedules are published daily in the free *Notícias da Madeira* newspaper, available at hotels.

Look out, too, for the screenings of more serious films at the Teatro Municipal located on Avenida Arriaga, which is opposite the Tourist Information Office.

Discotheques

The most popular are given below:

Copa Cabana
Carlton Park Hotel. Tel: (291) 231121.

Jose Braga Sousa
Rua Conde Canavia 19.
Tel: (291) 223518.

O Farol
Madeira Carlton. Tel: (291) 231031.

Vespas
*Avenida Sá Carneiro. Tel: (291) 231202.
Open: nightly 11pm–4am.*

Fado

It is difficult to account for the enormous popularity of *fado* (meaning 'fate'), the plaintive Portuguese music and song that tells of tragic events, dark destinies and lost loves, yet popular it is, and there are plenty of opportunities to wallow in an evening of soulful fatalism. Madeirans highly rate performances at:

Arsenio's Restaurant
Rua de Santa Maria 169. Tel: (291) 224007. Open: daily noon–2am.

Marcelino Fado House
*Travessa da Torre 22A, Zona Velha (Old Town). Tel: (291) 230834.
Open: daily 10.30pm–4am.*

O Pitéu Bar and Restaurant
*Rua da Carreira 182A. Tel: (291) 220819.
Open: Tue, Fri & Sat.*

Traditional Portuguese *fado* musicians

Music and Dance

Madeira's traditional music and dance makes light of the heavy burdens of work and slavery. In one very distinctive dance the participants turn in slow circles with their heads bowed, taking short steps as if their feet were chained together. It is called the Dance of Ponta do Sol, named after the area where Moorish and African slaves were kept during the early days of the island's colonisation. Similar in style are the Carrier's Dance, representing heavily laden peasants jogging along the island's footpaths beneath stacks of sugar cane or baskets loaded with bananas, and the Heavy Dance, in which the regular rhythmic stamping is said to reflect the custom of crushing grapes with bare feet to make Madeira wine. Madeiran song is more lighthearted and tells of courtship, the pleasures of the autumn harvest and the joys of wine. In contrast the *charamba* is a kind of musical duel, with a lively chorus, in which two singers improvise alternative verses which satirise the other person's looks, character or reputation, to the amusement of the audience.

Musical accompaniment to both song and dance is provided by the four-stringed *braguinha*, similar to a ukulele, wooden castanets called *castanholas,* and a notched stick called a *raspadeira*, decorated with a carved head and played like a washboard.

Most intriguing of all is the percussive

brinquinho, a hand-held pole where dolls in Madeiran costume wearing bells and castanets slide up and down in rhythm with the music.

Madeira still has numerous folklore groups who perform at festivals all round the island, dedicated to keeping Madeira's traditions alive. They can also be seen at folklore evenings hosted by Funchal's major hotels and at the **Café Relogio** restaurant in Camacha most evenings (*tel: (291) 922777*).

The Madeiran song and dance traditions are handed down by each generation

Children

As a destination, Madeira tends to attract older visitors rather than young families, so there are fewer facilities for children than you would find in other Portuguese resorts, such as the Algarve. If you do bring your children, though, you can be sure of a warm reception wherever you go because the Madeirans themselves are very indulgent towards the young.

Playing in the park . . .

If your children swim and are old enough to be trusted on their own, they will happily spend hours at the pool. The **Lido Complex** (*see p156*), located in the Hotel Zone on Rua do Gorgulho, is by far the best pool on Madeira and is preferable to the handkerchief-sized pools that most hotels squeeze on to their terraces or rooftops. The drawback is that it is packed with people at the weekend, so the best time to take your children is during the week. In contrast,

several of the larger hotels have sports facilities that are underused – your children could be encouraged to spend a few hours on the tennis courts, enjoy a few rounds of crazy golf, or bash hell out of a table-tennis ball.

Of the museums in Funchal, the **Museu Municipal** (*see p50*) will probably prove the most appealing, both for the stuffed sharks and other monsters of the deep upstairs, and for the real live fish, crabs and lobsters in the small downstairs aquarium.

Gorgeously coloured tropical birds can be seen at the **Jardim dos Loiros** (*see p42*), and there is a small 'zoo' in

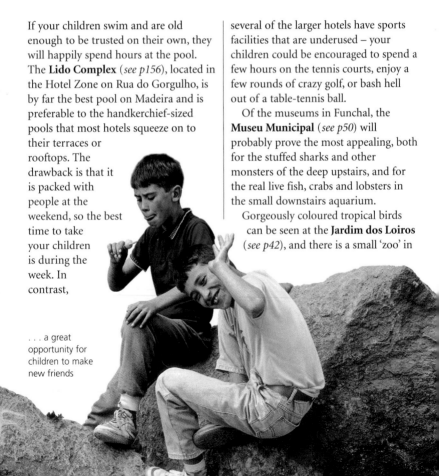
. . . a great opportunity for children to make new friends

Many places offer a small paddling pool for children as an alternative to the main pool

the public gardens in Santo da Serra, featuring deer, birds of prey and a kangaroo. Neither of these will absorb your children's attention for very long, however, and those who are attuned to environmental issues may well be repelled by the conditions in which the animals and birds are kept.

Younger children can burn off energy in the small playground in the **Jardim de Santa Catarina** park (*see pp42–3*) which has swings, climbing frames and plenty of space to run around in, and they will probably find it as much fun to watch the antics of the scurrying wall lizards, or chase the large butterflies with their tissue-paper wings.

Walking by the seafront is another way to spend some time. There are always boats to see in Funchal's yachting marina and sometimes huge ocean-going cruisers, as well as working ships stacked with containers. The marina waters are surprisingly clean and clear and you can watch shoals of silvery fish, some quite large, darting and turning in the sun-warmed waters.

Come night-time, your children might enjoy some of the shows put on by the hotels, though these are mostly aimed at an older audience.

If all else fails, there is always television, and MTV, the music channel, can be relied upon for the usual non-stop pop videos.

Sport and Leisure

Quite a number of Madeira's visitors come with the idea of getting some gentle exercise and keeping fit, so the better hotels all have pools and tennis courts. The island has two golf courses, both in spectacular settings, and though it lacks beaches, there is plenty of scope for watersports, including scuba-diving and fishing (*see p133*).

Tennis at the Quinta do Magnólia

Hotel Facilities

If sports are your priority then it is worth choosing your hotel based on the facilities it offers. Five-star seafront hotels such as the **Hotel Savoy Classic**, **Madeira Palacio**, **Pestana Carlton Madeira**, **Reid's** and the **Pestana Carlton Park Resort & Casino** have tennis courts and swimming pools large enough for serious work outs.

The **Hotel Savoy Classic** (*tel: (291) 775936*) has the best seafront complex of all the hotels, there is access to windsurfing, sailing, sea-canoeing, miniature golf and a putting green along with a fitness centre and tennis courts. The **Pestana Carlton Park Resort & Casino** (*tel: (291) 209100*) offers a high technology fitness centre, whirlpool and tennis.

Guests are given first priority to the hotels amenities and using the facilities but most hotels will admit non-residents for an admission fee. Something to inquire about is if the hotel will waive the admission fee if you dine there.

The Lido Complex

For serious swimmers and for families with children, the Municipal Lido Complex, on Rua do Gorgulho, offers a good alternative to hotel facilities. The complex includes an Olympic-size pool, a children's pool, access to the sea from a diving platform, solariums and several cafés and restaurants.

Open daily from 8.30am to 8pm in summer and 9am to 6pm in winter, the Lido is well worth visiting during the week, but with 3,000 visitors packed into the complex at weekends, it can seem unbearably overcrowded.

Quinta do Magnólia

Madeira's other public facility is the elegant **Quinta do Magnolia** (*tel: (291) 764598*) on Rua Dr. Pita. Formerly the British Country Club, the quinta's palm-filled gardens, with public pool, tennis courts, jogging track and playground, offer a quiet oasis in a busy part of Funchal. *The grounds are open daily 8am–9.30pm.*

The building now houses the **Biblioteca de Cultural Estrangeiros** (Foreign Culture Library), *tel: (291) 233164; email: americancorner@ mail.telepac.pt. Open: Mon–Fri 9am–5.30pm.* The library has an excellent supply of international books that anyone can borrow for free.

Golf

Madeira has two golf courses, both noted for their magnificent views and picturesque setting. The older one is the 27-hole **Santo da Serra** course (*tel: (291) 550100*), set high at 6,015m on a plateau to the east of the island. This is the venue for the Madeira Open tournament, held every January, which attracts many top international players.

The newer course is the 18-hole **Palheiro Golf** (*tel: (291) 790126*), situated high above Funchal at 6,015m and carved out of the 324-hectare Quinta do Palheiro estate. The views are enhanced by the surrounding woodland, much of it planted by the Blandy family since they acquired the estate in 1885 (*see pp102–3*).

Horse Riding

Contact the Associacao Hipica da Madeira, *Quinta Vila Alpires, Camhino dos Pretos, Sao Joao de Latrao (tel: (291) 792582)* which is open Tue 3–6pm, Wed–Sun 10am–1pm & 3–6pm. Arrangements can also be made at the Hotel Estrelicia on Caminho Velha da Ajuda (*tel: (219) 706600*).

Football

Madeirans are passionate about football; they claim the game was introduced to Portugal via Madeira, and that's quite likely given the island's long-standing relationship with Britain. The **Estádio dos Barreiros** stadium, whose concrete bulk looms north of the Hotel Zone, is home to Madeira's first division team, CS Marítimo, which plays on alternate Sunday afternoons in the season.

Football is a family affair and there is no risk of violence. The stadium stands high above Funchal, so, as the locals say, if there's not much happening on the field, you can always enjoy the view.

The Santo da Serra golf course

Food and Drink

Madeira's mild climate allows dining alfresco any time of day year round. Most restaurants have patios or rooftop terraces. The food is fresh and, for the most part, inexpensive. Dining in the hotels will offer more choices, but it can be pricey. For good value dine in the smaller restaurants and cafés in Funchal, or, better yet, outside the city. You might try *marisqueiras* restaurants specialising in seafood, or *churrascarias* that serve grilled foods.

Madeira is known for the quality of wine produced

Wherever you dine ambience and location should count a great deal in your decision. For location there is the Hotel Zone with its well-stocked five-star hotel restaurants where you will find the largest and priciest choices of international *haute cuisine* as well as excellent Italian, Chinese and Indian restaurants.

For atmosphere go where Madeirans go, the **centre**, where you will find a plethora of restaurants offering traditional foods such as garlic prawns, grilled tuna and plank steaks.

If you are a seafood fanatic, then the restaurants lining Funchal's yacht marina are the best bet. Here you can select crabs or lobsters live from the tank or choose from a vast range of shellfish or grilled fresh fish – and look out on to magnificent views of the mast-filled marina while you eat.

Further east, many of the pavement cafés of the Zona Velha (Old Town) offer the cheapest prices in Funchal and a festive, youthful atmosphere that is particularly appealing at weekends in summer when some cafés lay on musical entertainment and the party goes on well into the night.

Prices

It is easy to eat well and cheaply on Madeira if you eat local food and drink local wines. The prices begin to rise as soon as you go for anything imported. Don't forget, too, that some dishes, especially seafood and fish, are priced according to weight and by the prevailing market price: before you order what may be an expensive out-of-season fish, check with the waiter to get an idea of what a portion will cost.

In most Madeiran restaurants you will not have to order a side dish. The main entrées are usually served with fresh salads and boiled potatoes, staples everywhere on the island.

The star ratings in the restaurant listings below have been used to indicate the approximate cost per person in euros of a two-course meal with alcohol and a coffee:

★	Up to €10
★★	€10–15
★★★	€15–30
★★★★	More than €30

Where to Eat

Hotel Zone

Bamboo Inn ★★★
Smart and efficient Chinese restaurant making good use of Madeira's plentiful supply of fresh fish and vegetables. An excellent alternative to the local cuisine.
Estrada Monumental 318, 2nd Floor.
Tel: (291) 766861.

Beerhouse ★
Pub-style snack restaurant and bar.
Sao Lazaro, Porto do Funchal.
Tel: (291) 229011.

Casa dos Reis ★★★
Intimate restaurant behind the Savoy Hotel, serving French and international cuisine.
Rua da Penha de França 6.
Tel: (291) 225182.

Casa Velha ★★★★
Elegant dining in a well-restored 19th-century town house; specialises in *flambé* dishes and lobster with pasta.
Rua Imperatriz Dona Amélia 69.
Tel: (291) 221388.

Doca do Cavacas ★★
Atmospheric restaurant specialising in seafood and fresh fish.
Ponta da Cruz, Estrada Monumental.
Tel: (291) 762057.

Dona Amélia ★★★★
Elegant but pricey international-standard cuisine, set in a restored 19th-century town house with intimate terrace.
Rua Imperatriz Dona Amélia 83.
Tel: (291) 225784.

Don Filet ★★★
Brazilian-style charcoal-grilled beef plus local *espetada* kebabs and piano music.
Rua do Favila 7, by the Savoy Hotel.
Tel: (291) 237848.

Novelty dining at Funchal's harbourside floating restaurant complex

Eye-catching signage

Escola Profissional de Hotelaria ★★★★
Dine where Madeira's future chefs and waiters receive their exemplary training. The hotel school serves lunch, high tea and dinner. All expertly prepared and elegantly served by advance-level students.
Travessa dos Piornais.
Tel: (291) 700386.
Dress: smart casual.
Reservations essential.

Fleur-de-Lys ★★★★
The Savoy Hotel's flagship restaurant; top quality international cuisine, impeccable service and panoramic views over Funchal and the harbour.
Savoy Hotel, Avenida do Infante.
Tel: (291) 228255.
Reservations essential.

Hong Kong ★★
Authentic Cantonese food and decor.
Olimpo Shopping Centre, Avenida do Infante.
Tel: (291) 228181.

Les Faunes ★★★★
Probably Madeira's best restaurant, the haunt of visiting dignitaries and those who can afford a very special night out. The bright and airy dining room is simply decorated with drawings of fauns by Picasso. Formal evening dress is not compulsory but is worn by most of the guests.
Reid's Hotel, Estrada Monumental.
Tel: (291) 717100.
Reservations advised.

Moby Dick ★★
Situated near the ocean and the main road in an ugly courtyard between Reid's and the Lido, this not very pretty café is surprisingly good. The interior makes up for what the exterior lacks. And the food is excellent; seafood such as *gambus piri piri* (spiced prawns), vegetarian choices and what many consider to be the freshest fish in Funchal. An added plus, if you are not staying nearby: the owner will pick you up (minimum four people).
Estrada Monumental 87.
Tel: (291) 776868.

Reid's Dining Room ★★★★
Slightly less expensive than Les Faunes, but equally smart (evening dress advised), Reid's main dining room offers chandeliered elegance and a choice of reasonably priced set menus or more highly priced à la carte.
Reid's Hotel, Estrada Monumental.
Tel: (291) 763001.
Dinner only. Reservations essential.

Sol e Mar ★★
A lively and informal, good value restaurant offering pizza, pasta, *flambé* or Madeiran dishes, including the just-has-to-be-sampled fish stew.
Flor do Lido Building, Estrada Monumental 314B. Tel: (291) 762227.

Summertime ★★
Great value for families with its location near the Lido complex making it a rest break from swimming, with lunches and dinners of good

quality Portuguese dishes. Grown ups will enjoy the terrace overlooking the ocean.
Estrada Monumental 21.
Tel: (291) 762467.
Villa Cliff ★★
Adjoining Reid's Hotel. recommended for imaginative pasta dishes.
Estrada Monumental 169.
Tel: (291) 763025.

Downtown Funchal
O Almirante ★★★
A very romantic, candle-lit interior makes up for the traffic-laden front terrace. The dining room has an old world feel with exposed wooden beams, chandeliers and high-

backed chairs. The food and service are traditional and exquisite; dine on dishes such as *Fidago ao Madeira* (Madeira liver), lobster, squid and shark.
Largo do Poco 1–2.
Tel: (291) 224252.
Arsénio's ★★
Pizza and fish restaurant, popular for its live *fado* singing and music.
Rua de Santa Maria 169.
Tel: (291) 224007.
Café Esplenada Arco-Velho ★
The best of a run of pavement cafés in the Old Town. Friendly service and a good choice of authentic local dishes at rock-bottom prices.

Rua de Carlos I, 42.
Tel: (291) 225683.
Caravelha ★★★
Smart *flambé* restaurant with harbour views and one of the few in Madeira to offer a specific vegetarian menu. Seafood risotto (*arroz de mariscos*) is also a popular choice.
Avenida do Mar 15.
Tel: (291) 223695.
O Celeiro ★★★
Smart cellar restaurant, ideal for a romantic candle-lit dinner, serving fresh grilled fish, traditional Madeiran dishes and the southern Portuguese speciality of *cataplana de mariscos* (seafood casserole).

Packed with choice, the Old Town

Nautical decor promising fresh fish

Rua dos Aranhas 22.
Tel: (291) 230622.
Golfinho ★★
Portholes and ships'
wheels give this Old Town
restaurant its nautical
flavour, and ships'
lanterns provide
atmospheric light at
night. The Golfinho
specialises in fresh
seafood but also serves
good value beef and
chicken dishes.
Largo do Corpo Santo 21.
Tel: (291) 226774.

O Jango ★★★
A tiny Old Town
restaurant which only
seats 20 customers. It
specialises in *arroz de*
mariscos (seafood rice)
and *cataplana*, a hearty
fish stew.
Rua de Santa Maria 166.
Tel: (291) 221840.
Reservations essential.

Le Jardin ★★
Old Town restaurant
with French influences,
specialising in *flambé* fish
and peppered steak.
Rua de Carlos I, 60.
Tel: (291) 222864.

Londres ★★
Despite the name,
authentic Madeiran and
mainland Portuguese
cuisine is served here,
with a different speciality
each day of the week – a
good place to sample

bacalhau (salt cod) for
which it is said there are
as many recipes as
there are days in the year.
Rua da Carreira 64A.
Tel: (291) 35329.
Closed: Sun.

Marina Terrace ★★
Pizza, seafood and live
entertainment with sea
views. One of several
good restaurants fronting
the yacht marina, serving
everything from pizza to
lobster. Staff wear
Madeiran costume and
there is live music and
folk-dancing nightly from
around 7.30pm.
Marina do Funchal.
Tel: (291) 230547.

Marisa ★★

Another family owned restaurant known for its Portuguese specialities, this one's are *paella, arroz di marisco* (seafood rice), spicy prawns and grilled beef. A small wooden balcony upstairs allows for alfresco dining. It is very small so plan to call ahead.
Rua de Santa Maria 22. Tel: (291) 226189.

Portao ★★

Famous for its fish, meat and *bacalhau* (salt cod) dishes, the restaurant's tables spill out on to the terrace near the church making this a great place to people watch. Service is so friendly that by the end of the evening everyone will know your name.
Rua do Portao de Sao Tiago.

Tartaruga

If you get a yearning for sausages, beans, chips and eggs then head over to this tiny family run place with a few tables jammed inside and more overflowing on to the terrace facing the Carmo church. The owner's father used to sell turtle shells here; *tartaruga* means 'turtle shell', now the son and his Scottish-born wife

offer inexpensive Portuguese and Scottish fare to patrons.
Largo do Corpo Santo 4–6.

Vagrant ★★

Also known as 'The Beatles' Boat' because it was once owned by the famous four, this now forms the centrepiece of Funchal's so-called 'Floating Restaurant' area; but do not worry if you suffer from sea sickness – these boats are firmly bedded in concrete and their floating days are well and truly over. Despite the gimmicky ambience, you can eat well here on pizza or typical Madeiran food at reasonable prices.
Avenida do Mar.

Pavement cafés abound on the island

What to Eat

It may seem that Madeiran menus are deliberately designed to confuse non-Portuguese visitors. Three of the most popular dishes all have very similar names: *espada* (scabbard fish), *espetada* (beef kebabs) and *espadarte* (swordfish). Learn the difference between these three, and you will have the key to eating well during your stay.

Espada

Espada are the rather ugly-looking elongated fish that you will see for sale in the Mercado dos Lavradores (Workers' Market) in Funchal. The name *espada* means 'scabbard', referring to their long flat shape. Once cleaned and prepared for cooking they look innocuous enough, but in the market their long snout, vicious teeth and over-large eyes are the stuff of nightmares.

In fact, *espada* are very unusual fish, unique to the waters around Madeira and to certain islands in Japan. They live at very great depths – below 800m, hence their large eyes, necessary for seeing in the gloom. They are

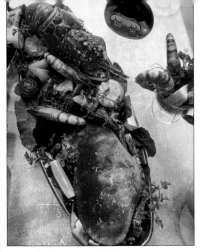
The seafood gourmet's delight

carnivorous, hence the razor-sharp teeth, and they rise to 500m at night to feed, which is when Madeira's fishermen make their catch, using long lines with up to 150 hooks baited with squid. Decompression kills the fish before they reach the surface and their meat is very versatile: in authentic Madeiran restaurants it is likely to be served *com banana* (fried in butter with a slice of banana on top) or *com vinho e alhos* (marinaded in wine and vinegar before being fried in olive oil); in tourist restaurants it is more likely to be served with white wine sauce and prawns.

Espetada

Espetada consists of chunks of beef, skewered on a stick made from the fresh green wood of the bay tree, which imparts flavour to the meat as it cooks. The meat is rolled in chopped garlic, sea salt and crushed bay leaves, and traditionally the kebabs are grilled over the embers of a fire made from vine prunings, which adds another subtle layer of flavouring. This dish, once reserved for special festivities, such as

Espada: ugly but delicious

Christmas and the Feast of the Assumption, is now the staple of Madeiran restaurant menus, where it is often cooked under an electric grill and thus lacks the genuine taste of wood-cooked meat. At some rural restaurants, such as the **Abrigo do Poiso** (*tel: (291) 782269*), located at Poiso (*see p96*) on the road between Funchal and Faial, you can watch *espetada* being cooked the traditional way, on an open fire, and savour the difference. To accompany the meat, chips and salad are usually served, and in traditional restaurants chunks of *bolo de caco*. This country bread is made from nothing but flour, sweet potatoes and a small amount of yeast and water; allowed to prove for 24 hours, it is then shaped into flat circles and cooked quickly on top of a flat stone heated in the same open fire used to cook the kebabs. The result is a spongy open-textured bread with a delicious crust.

Espadarte and Other Fish

Espadarte, or swordfish, is one of several big and meaty fish that you will find on the menu in restaurants specialising in fish and seafood. Others include *pargo* (bream), s*almonet*e (red mullet) and *atum* (tuna), usually served grilled with onion sauce and accompanied by *milho frito*, deep-fried cubes of maize flour mixed with cabbage and herbs.

Nearly all fish restaurants serve seafood paella (*arroz de mariscos*) because it is such a spectacular dish, garlanded with prawns and decked with all kinds of shellfish, but the dish and its ingredients are imported for the sake of visitors and it is likely to be expensive. If you want to go native, then try *bacalhau a gomes de sá* (salt cod casseroled with onions, potatoes, garlic and olives, and garnished with chopped boiled eggs) or *caldeirada*, a tasty fish stew made from fish, potatoes, onions and tomatoes.

Espetada: traditionally grilled over the aromatic wood of vines or bay trees

The Madeiran Menu

As soon as you are seated at any good Madeiran café or restaurant table, the waiter is likely to present you with a plate of warm bread dripping with garlic butter. Hoping that the garlic will counterbalance the cholesterol effects of the butter, you can enjoy this deliciously simple food while pondering the menu.

Starters

The most typical Madeiran starters are grilled limpets and tomato soup. With limpets (*lapas*) you risk pushing the cholesterol count even higher, since they are often served in the shell in a puddle of melted garlic butter, but these are the only native Madeiran shellfish – everything else is imported. Far healthier is *sopa de tomate* made from finely chopped onions and tomatoes with a lightly poached egg added to each person's bowl before serving.

Dark and spice-rich *bolo de mel* (honey cake)

Main Courses and Side Dishes

All main courses (*see pp164–5*) come with potatoes (boiled with fish, chips with meat) and salad or vegetables, so you do not need to order any side dishes unless you wish. If you do order a side dish, make it clear you want it served at the same time as the main course, otherwise it will be presented on its own, after the starter.

Desserts

Rarely will you be offered much of a choice. Ice cream is ubiquitous but you may be offered fruit salad – if this is fresh it can be delicious, incorporating the best of the island's tropical varieties, such as papaya, passion fruit, mangoes and custard apples.

Grilled limpets in garlic-flavoured butter

Drinks

Coral beer is brewed on Madeira and is a light refreshing lager with a flowery fragrance. Madeiran table wine is also very drinkable but it is hard to find in Funchal, despite laws requiring bars and restaurants to offer it on their wine lists. Restaurateurs make more money from selling expensive imported wines; if you ask for local wine you are quite likely to be told 'it's not very nice'. In reality, the local wine is light, refreshing, only just fermented, and as much like grape juice in character as wine. Look out for what the locals drink.

Among imported wines, chilled and slightly sparkling *vinho verde* (young or 'green' wine) is a reliable choice to accompany fish, and the robust oaky reds from Dão and Bairrada reveal their rich character when drunk with meat.

Coffee on Madeira is continental in style – you will be served an *espresso* (*bica* in Portuguese) unless you request otherwise. With it you could try one of Madeira's numerous liqueurs: *maracujá* (made from passion fruit, and said to be an excellent aphrodisiac), *ginja* (made from cherries) and *licor de castanha* (distilled from sweet chestnuts).

Snacks

Madeira's staple lunchtime sandwich is the *prego no prato*, made from country bread spread with garlic butter and enclosing a chunk of grilled steak, a robust and filling energy-reviver served in traditional bars or cafés. Vegetarians have a harder time, but new-style cafés such as Vivaldi (*Rua da Figueira Preta 6, just off Rua 31 de Janeiro. Tel: (291) 222028*) are beginning to appear,

offering delicatessen-style salads and gourmet sandwiches, plus very good home-made ice cream.

Another staple is *bolo do mel* (honey cake), sold in every *pastelaria* (baker's shop). Traditionally made at Christmas but consumed all year, this dark, fruit-filled, spicy cake contains many ingredients – but honey is not one of them; the sweetness comes from the hot molasses added to the cake dough before it is cooked, a legacy of Madeira's ancient sugar-cane industry.

Sugar-cane spirit, drunk with lemon and honey

Hotels and Accommodation

Madeira offers a wide choice in quality accommodation, ranging from venerable old hotels such as Reid's (*see pp170–1*) to inexpensive self-catering apartments. Package holiday prices are hard to beat but you must book well in advance if you want to visit during the time school holidays are on, remembering that Madeira is as popular in winter as in summer: in fact, Christmas and New Year are the most expensive times to visit because of the festivities (*see pp20–1*).

An old mansion converted to an elegant small hotel

If you do book a package to Madeira, be sure to compare operators' prices because they vary quite a lot, even for identical rooms in the same hotel. Be careful, too, to check how far out of town the hotel is situated – some are up to 5km from the city centre, and though they offer a shuttle bus service, you will still feel isolated. On the other hand, these hotels are often cheaper to stay in. Keep in mind that rates vary markedly according to the season.

Five-star Hotels

All five-star establishments in Funchal occupy prime positions in the Hotel Zone, are less than ten minutes' walk from the city centre, have splendid sea views, huge swimming pools and direct access to the sea with roped-off bathing areas. You will be charged approximately €115–150 per night, plus a supplement for a room with a sea view, but you may consider this worthwhile since rooms without sea views look on to the busy Estrada Monumental.

Three- and Four-star Hotels

Most of the island's hotels fall into this category and are located in the sprawl of high-rise developments stretching westwards from the city centre along the Estrada Monumental.

Nearly all the hotels have a pool, but rarely big enough for serious swimming, though the excellent Lido pool complex (*see* Sport, *pp156–7*) is located in the midst of the Hotel Zone, and the area is well supplied with shops and restaurants. Nearly all the hotels are modern, and for approximately €55–80 per night, you can usually count on your own balcony and bathroom, satellite TV, direct-dial telephones, plus a café, bar and small shop. Breakfast is nearly always included in the room price: this can range from tea or coffee, a bread roll and fruit, to a sumptuous buffet spread.

Quinta-style Hotels

Many elegant *quintas* (or mansions) were demolished to make way for the high-rises of the Hotel Zone, but thankfully, others have survived and a few have been converted into elegant, antique-filled hotels set in well-tended gardens – worth seeking out if you are an incurable romantic with a pocket to match.

Self-catering

Funchal has many inexpensive apartments and aparthotels where the accommodation includes a small kitchen and a living/eating area – excellent if you want to take children or prepare your own meals. Private apartments with maid service are also available; look for classified advertisements in the travel sections of the weekend newspapers.

Budget Accommodation

No-frills accommodation for about €25–50 per night is available in *pensãos* (pensions), often located above shops, bars or restaurants. The setting is not always tranquil, but the prices are very

reasonable and ideal for anyone travelling on a tight budget.

Beyond Funchal

Several towns along Madeira's southern coast have resort complexes, with a mix of hotels and apartments, which some visitors use as an alternative base for exploring the island, especially those who want to escape from the city and enjoy relative solitude. The island also has two *pousadas*, state-owned hotels, deliberately sited in isolated positions and popular with walkers. The 18-room Pousada do Pico do Arieiro (*tel: (291) 230110*) is located at the summit of Madeira's third highest peak and is perfect for those who want to experience the silence of the mountains, the beauty of the night sky, and the glowing light of the rising sun. The other hotel is the Pousada dos Vinháticos, at Serra da Água (*tel: (291) 952344*). Both need booking several days in advance, longer if you want to stay at the weekend.

Five-star luxury: Madeira's best hotels all have large seafront swimming pools

Reid's Hotel

Reid's is one of those legendary hotels which nearly everyone has heard of, the sort of place which regularly entertains Hollywood film stars, royalty and heads of state. In rags-to-riches fashion, the hotel was founded by William Reid, one of 12 children of

an impoverished Scottish crofter. Reid set off in 1836 to make his fortune, and worked his passage on board ship to Madeira, where he met William Wilkinson. Together they set up an agency catering to the needs of Madeira's wealthy foreign visitors, most of whom would hire a *quinta* (a large house and garden) for the duration of their stay, relying on Reid to find a suitable property and furnish it according to their tastes. The money Reid made enabled him to buy *quintas* and convert them into residential hotels; eventually he bought the plot of land on which Reid's Hotel now sits, enjoying a prime cliff-top position with wonderful sea views.

William Reid did not live to see his dream fulfilled – he died in 1888, aged 66, while the hotel was under construction – but his sons took over and opened the doors of this luxury hotel to the first paying guests in 1891. British Prime Minister Winston Churchill was just one of the many regular guests who would arrive by sea at the hotel's private landing stage, to be carried by lift to the upper gardens, immaculately tended and filled with palms. The hotel buildings resemble a cross between a colonial gentlemen's club and an aristocrat's home.

Even if you cannot afford to stay at Reid's, you can still enjoy the hushed ambience and impeccable service by splashing out on afternoon tea (Madeira cake and cucumber sandwiches with the crusts removed). The poolside buffet lunch is another way of taking in the hotel's style, or you can sip Madeira in the cocktail bar. Just remember to dress smartly, though, or you might be politely turned away – the hotel no longer insists that evening dress be worn for dinner, but it does suggest that you might feel conspicuous if you do not.

Reid's is proud of its traditional values; luxury cruise passengers arrive by boat at the hotel's private landing stage and are carried by lift up the cliffs to their rooms
Above: tea on the balcony with an unrivalled view

On Business

Tourism remains Madeira's principal income earner, with wine, flowers, fruit, embroidery and basketry as the main exports. These are relatively mature industries, with little scope for growth in the future, although tourism still offers plenty of opportunities for small entrepreneurs to enter the market and offer new services.

One of the many local banks in Madeira

Recognising the need to diversify, the Madeiran government has set up the Zona Franca Industrial, a duty-free industrial zone, in the east of the island, near Caniçal. The idea is that manufacturers should be able to import raw materials and export finished goods without paying any taxes and levies, but the project is in its infancy and is relatively small scale.

Madeira also has quite a sophisticated banking system, thanks to the large number of so-called 'emigrants' who leave the island to work abroad but who remit their foreign currency earnings home, or who return to Madeira after a number of years with a substantial nest egg. This banking expertise, combined with the fact that Madeira is free to make its own fiscal laws, has led some commentators to speculate whether Madeira might not develop into an offshore banking haven for Europe.

Emigrants

The wealth of some Madeiran emigrants is the stuff of island legends. Some made their fortunes working in oil-rich

Excellent conference facilities make it possible to combine business and pleasure

A potential offshore banking haven

Venezuela while others built up retail or restaurant businesses in Africa and Asia. One of the best-known examples is Manuel Pestana, who emigrated to South Africa in the 1940s and made his fortune selling beer, wines and spirits. His son, Dionísio, now heads the Pestana Group, which owns the Madeira Carlton and Carlton Park hotels and has major interests in hotels, aviation and real estate.

Business Culture

The Pestana family typify the entrepreneurship that characterises most Madeirans, and in theory doing business in Madeira ought to be relatively straightforward. In practice, people who have experience of the Madeiran business culture report that it is very difficult to make headway without the involvement of local Madeiran partners. As a first step, the local Chamber of Commerce provides information and introductions:

Câmara de Comércio e Indústria da Madeira
Avenida Arriaga 41. Tel: (291) 230137.

Conferences

All the features which make Madeira a good holiday destination also make it a popular place to hold conferences. All of the five-star hotels offer facilities, but the Madeira Carlton and the Carlton Park Hotel both have purpose-designed conference centres and host most of the prestigious international trade fairs and conferences.

The Pestana Carlton Park Resort & Casino Funchal
Rua Imperatiz Dona Amelia.
Tel: (291) 209100.

Pestana Madeira Carlton
Largo Antonio Nobre.
Tel: (291) 239500.

Practical Guide

Arriving
Passports
The rules for entering Madeira are the same as those for the Portuguese mainland: citizens of other European Union (EU) member states and those from the USA, Canada, Australia and New Zealand can stay for up to 60 days without a visa. You will need to show your passport on entry; you will also need it when registering at hotels or changing money and traveller's cheques.

Travellers who require visas should obtain them in their country of residence, as it may prove difficult to obtain them elsewhere.

By Air
The cheapest way to get to Madeira is by chartered flight. Tour operators and handling agents (Triam, Servisair and TAP) specialising in Madeira offer direct flights to Funchal as part of a hotel and flight package, but many of them also offer inexpensive flight-only deals using their in-house charter aircraft.

Camping at Porto Moniz

TAP (Air Portugal), the national carrier, also offers scheduled flights direct to Funchal as well as via Lisbon. These flights are more expensive but you can fly any day of the week. To compete with charter carriers, TAP often runs special schemes involving free car rental or the option to stop in Lisbon at no extra cost.

Airport Facilities
Funchal's Santa Catarina airport is small and efficient, and lies 18km outside the city. You will rarely experience delays except in very severe weather; even this is less of a problem because the runway was upgraded and extended in 1990, allowing much larger planes to use the airport. There is a viewing platform on the roof of the terminal building and all the usual airport facilities: a small duty-free shop, a currency exchange bureau, several car hire agencies plus bars and cafés.

City Link
Transport from the airport to your hotel is usually included in package tours. If not, there are taxis available just outside the terminal exit doors to get to central Funchal. There is a very cheap bus that calls at the airport at regular intervals throughout the day. The drive to Funchal takes 20–30 minutes by taxi, 60 minutes by bus.

By Sea
There are no ferry services to Madeira, but British, Russian and Norwegian cruise liners regularly visit the island as

part of a week-long tour of the Canary Islands, Madeira and North Africa. Cruise passengers rarely get more than 24 hours on Madeira, scarcely long enough to sample the island's varied attractions, but some cruise companies allow you to take just part of the cruise, perhaps arriving in Madeira romantically by sea and returning home by air.

Camping

Officially, camping in the mountains and forests is illegal on Madeira. There are two designated campsites on the island; **Parque de Campismo Porto Moniz** (*tel: (291) 850193 or (291) 853447*) and **Parque de Campismo Porto Santo** (*tel: (291) 982160) or (291) 982361*). Both are inexpensive and very basic; a piece of grass to pitch your tent, loos and cold showers only. These campsites have limited space, best to book well in advance if planning to visit in July and August.

Children

For advice on enjoying Madeira with children, *see pp154–5*.

Climate

Funchal has an almost perfect climate; temperatures do not vary much from an average of 22°C throughout the year, making it a perfect place to escape from the cold of northern European winters or the excessive heat of summer. Funchal and other towns on the south side of the island receive very little rain, except in autumn. The weather on the rest of the island is variable, depending on altitude and aspect with the north

receiving most of the rain, and rain-clouds hanging almost permanently at the 800–1,000m level (*see pp8–9 for further information*).

Conversion Tables

See p177.
Clothes and shoe sizes in Madeira follow the standard sizes used in the rest of Europe.

Crime

Crime is an evil that has yet to take root in Madeira. Within the island's close-knit communities still strongly influenced by the teachings of the Roman Catholic church, serious crimes are so rare as to be profoundly shocking when they occur. Even so, you should not offer an invitation to crime by being careless with your valuables; use your hotel safe and do not leave possessions in unattended cars.

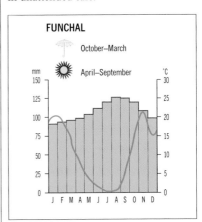

FUNCHAL

October–March

April–September

| mm | °C |

Weather Conversion Chart
25.4mm = 1 inch
°F = 1.8 x °C + 32

Do report crime at once if you fall victim to it – the police will do everything possible to help (*see* Police, *p183*).

Customs

As Madeira is part of the EU, visitors from its member countries benefit from new regulations introduced in 1993. The amount of duty-paid goods (those bought in local shops) you can take home from Madeira is only restricted by notional limits, above which you may be asked to prove that your purchases are for personal rather than commercial use.

If you are aged 17 or over you can bring back: 800 cigarettes, 400 cigarillos, 200 cigars, 1kg of tobacco, 90 litres of wine, 10 litres of spirits, 20 litres of fortified wine (or 26 bottles of Madeira) and 100 litres of beer.

As of 1999, duty-free allowances were abolished within the EU and travellers whose journey begins and ends in an EU country are no longer eligible. Visitors to Madeira from non-EU countries are still eligible.

The allowances here are (per person aged over 17): 200 cigarettes or 100 cigarillos or 50 cigars or 250g of tobacco; 1 litre of spirits or 2 litres of table wine and 2 litres of fortified or sparkling wine; 75cl of perfume.

These limits may vary from time to time so it is best to check when you make your purchase; current limits are posted in duty-free shops.

Driving

Renting a car gives you the flexibility to explore the island at your own pace. Bear in mind, though, that the daily cost

Women are well-represented in the police force

of car hire is about the same as hiring a taxi for the day, with the advantage that the taxi driver takes the strain of the island's steep and tortuous roads. Remember that if you do hire a car, the driver will see little of the countryside. The driver needs total concentration to avoid the myriad hazards; these include hairpin bends without crash barriers to prevent you plunging down the mountainsides, roads so narrow that only one car can pass, sheep and humans in the middle of the road and reckless Madeiran drivers.

A freeway which now extends from the airport, around Funchal, and as far as Ribeira Brava, makes driving a little easier. Most drivers are courteous, and they rarely break the speed limits of 60kph in built-up areas and 90kph elsewhere. Cars drive on the right, seat belts must be worn, and children under 12 are not allowed in the front seats. The more expensive hotels provide covered parking. Public car parks are located beneath the Marina Shopping Centre on Avenida do Mar and on the site of the old bus station near the Zona Velha. You pay by the hour, but the cost is reasonable. Outside Funchal free parking places are easy to find.

There are plenty of petrol stations in Funchal, including one that is open virtually around the clock on Avenida do Infante, nearly opposite the Carlton Park Hotel. It is a good idea to fill your tank before driving to the interior or north of the island where petrol stations are few and far between.

Warning triangles must be used if you break down, positioned in the road to the rear of the car. There are orange SOS call points at regular intervals beside main roads – walk to the nearest, press the button and wait for the rescue service to answer. Alternatively, car rental companies will give you a telephone number that you can use to call out their own rescue service.

Car Rental

If you do decide to explore Madeira at your own pace by car, be sure to book well in advance for the peak summer period (July, August and September), and for Christmas and New Year.

Look out too for the special 'Flydrive' packages organised by travel agencies which allow you to tour the island, staying in a different hotel every night, which include the cost of car rental.

To hire a car you must be over 21 years of age, with two years' driving

Conversion Table

FROM	TO	MULTIPLY BY
Inches	Centimetres	2.54
Feet	Metres	0.3048
Yards	Metres	0.9144
Miles	Kilometres	1.6090
Acres	Hectares	0.4047
Gallons	Litres	4.5460
Ounces	Grams	28.35
Pounds	Grams	453.6
Pounds	Kilograms	0.4536
Tons	Tonnes	1.0160

To convert back, for example from centimetres to inches, divide by the number in the third column.

Men's Suits

UK		36	38	40	42	44	46	48
Rest of Europe	46	48	50	52	54	56	58
USA		36	38	40	42	44	46	48

Dress Sizes

UK		8	10	12	14	16	18
France		36	38	40	42	44	46
Italy		38	40	42	44	46	48
Rest of Europe		34	36	38	40	42	44
USA		6	8	10	12	14	16

Men's Shirts

UK	14	14.5	15	15.5	16	16.5	17
Rest of Europe	36	37	38	39/40	41	42	43
USA	14	14.5	15	15.5	16	16.5	17

Men's Shoes

UK	7	7.5	8.5	9.5	10.5	11
Rest of Europe	41	42	43	44	45	46
USA	8	8.5	9.5	10.5	11.5	12

Women's Shoes

UK	4.5	5	5.5	6	6.5	7
Rest of Europe	38	38	39	39	40	41
USA	6	6.5	7	7.5	8	8.5

experience, a driving licence from your own country or an international driving licence, as well as a passport. You must keep your passport with you at all times while driving. Seat belts are to be worn at all times. Madeira has very strict laws on drinking and driving. Each car hire agency has their own policies regarding payment, but most will not accept cash and require a credit card.

Atlas Avda Infante 29, Funchal.
Tel: (291) 223100 Fax: (291) 741212.
Avis Santa Catalina Airport Funchal.
Tel: (291) 524392. www.avis.com
Largo Antonio Nobre 164 Funchal.
Tel: (291) 764546.
Hotel Monumental Lido Funchal.
Tel: (291) 764546.
Brava Car Caminho do Amparo 2.
Tel: (291) 764385.
Budget Santa Catalina Airport Funchal.
Tel: (291) 524661. www.budget.com
Hotel Duas Torres. Estrada Monumental 239 Funchal.
Tel: (291) 766518. Fax: (291) 765619.
Hertz Santa Catalina Airport Funchal.
Tel: (291) 523040. Fax: (291) 523017.
www.hertz.com

It is best to fill up petrol tanks before heading off the beaten track

Centro Comercial Lido Loja 1, Estrada Monumental Funchal.
Tel: (291) 764410. Fax: (291) 764452.
O Moinho Estrada Monumental.
Tel: (291) 762123.

Electricity
The standard supply on Madeira is 220 volts. Your appliance will work if it is fitted with a two-pin plug; otherwise an adaptor is needed.

Embassies and Consulates
UK Avda Zarco 2–4 Funchal.
Tel: (291) 212860.
USA Avda Luis de Camoes, Ed. Infante, Bloco B, AP. B–4 Funchal.
Tel: (291) 235636.

Emergency Numbers
Universal: *Tel: 112.*
Hospital(s): *Tel: (291) 705600 or (291) 705730.*

Health
Take care in the sun, whether out walking or by the pool. You can get burnt very quickly, as the sun is more intense than you think, despite the relatively low temperatures.

If you do have a health problem you can safely put yourself in the hands of the island's well-trained English-speaking doctors who have a long tradition of helping people who come to Madeira for medical care. Dr Zino (*Avenida do Infante 26. Tel: (291) 742227*) has a practice close to the Hotel Zone and is used by all tour operators.

If you seek medical treatment, remember to keep all bills and receipts in order to claim on your travel insurance policy. All EU countries have reciprocal arrangements for reclaiming the cost of medical services. UK residents should obtain the European Health Insurance Card from any UK post office. The card and your passport must be presented before treatment is sought at the **Serviço de Migrantes** (*Centro do Saúde de Bom Jesus, Rua das Hortas 67. Tel: (291) 229161. Open: Mon–Fri, 9.30am–noon & 2–4pm*).

Outside Funchal, nearly every community has a health centre (*Centro do Saúde*), where help can be sought, and there are emergency services (*urgência*) at the health centres in Ribeira Brava, Calheta, São Vicente, Porto Moniz, Santana and Machico. On Porto Santo, the centre is at Vila Baleira.

Madeira has no mandatory vaccination requirements, and no vaccination recommendations other than to keep tetanus and polio immunisation up to date. Like every other part of the world, AIDS is present.

The food and water on the island are safe to consume.

Lost Property
There is a good chance that any property you lose (especially if left in a taxi or bus) will be handed in to the lost property office in Funchal: contact **Polícia de Perdias & Achados** (*Rua João de Deus 7. Tel: (291) 222022*).

Maps
Perfectly adequate maps of Funchal and Madeira are given out free by the tourist office at *Avenida Arriaga 18, Funchal*. For walking, *The Landscapes of Madeira* (4th edition) by John and Pat

Underwood is the indispensable guide, with routes plotted on to Portuguese contoured military maps.

For driving, the Bartholomew *Madeira Holiday Map* is the most up to date, showing roads that are under construction and due to open in the years ahead.

In reading Madeiran maps, it is useful to know the meaning of certain place name elements:
achada plateau
arco curving mountain ridge
boca mouth/mountain pass
cabo cape
caldeirão crater or basin
calheta stream
caminho path and (confusingly) road
cruzinhas crossroads
encumeada summit
fonte spring
jardim garden
levada irrigation canal
lombada ridge
miradouro viewpoint
monte mount
parque park
praça square
ribeira river/river valley
rocha rock/crag
vale valley

Media
Madeira's main daily newspaper is the *Diário de Notícias*. This produces a four-page English-language supplement which is distributed to most hotels and which summarises local and world news. It also contains a miscellany of information on everything – from the weather, exchange rates, the day's TV and radio schedules, which cruise

LANGUAGE

Most Madeirans speak basic English and the staff of shops, hotels and restaurants will be fluent. It is worth knowing some basic Portuguese phrases, however, since you are likely to hear them spoken a lot, and you may even want to try them out yourself. Remember that in Portuguese, the letter s is pronounced like the s in sugar unless it is followed by a vowel; thus *carros* (car) is pronounced *carrosh*. The letter z sounds similar, so *faz favor* (please) is pronounced *fash favor*. When the tilde accent (~) appears above the letters ao (as in *pão* – bread) it sounds like ow followed by a slight oo (powoo).

USEFUL WORDS AND PHRASES

hello	olá
goodbye	adeus
good morning	bom dia
good afternoon	boa tarde
good evening	boa noite
please	faz favor
thank you	obrigada (F)
	obrigado (M)
yes/no	sim/não
do you speak English?	fala Inglês?
how are you?	como está?
very well	muito bem
how much?	quanta custa?
very good	muito bom
excuse me	com licença
sorry/pardon me	desculpe
it does not matter	não faz mal
good luck	boa sorte

IN BARS/CAFÉS

I would like (a beer)	queria (cerveja)
please	faz favor
Cheers (your health)	saúde
enjoy your meal	bom apetite
the bill please	a conta, faz favor
wine	vinho
house wine	vinho da casa
white	branco
red	tinto
rosé	rosé
green (young)	verde
sparkling	espumante
bottle	garrafa
half bottle	meia garrafa
tea	chá
lemon	limão
fizzy mineral water	água com gás
still mineral water	água sem gás
orange juice	sumo de laranja
coffee (espresso)	bica
coffee (large, strong and black)	café grande
coffee (large, weak and black)	carioca
coffee with milk (large cup) (literally 'a Chinese lady')	chinesa
coffee with milk (small cup)	garota
coffee with much milk (tall glass, literally 'a galleon')	galão
sugar	açúcar

FOOD	
breakfast	pequeno almoço
lunch	almoço
high tea (meal)	lanche
dinner	jantar
bread	pão
cake	bolo
cheese	queijo
chicken	frango
eggs	ovos
fish	peixe
fruit	fruta
ham	fiambre
ice cream	gelado
lamb	borrego
pork	porco
rice	arroz
shellfish	mariscos
steak	bife
tuna	átum
veal	vitela

OUT AND ABOUT	
airport	aeroporto
beach	praia
bus station	estação de autocarros
bus stop	paragem
cake shop	pastelaria
chemist	farmácia
church	igreja
danger	perigo/risco
doctor	médico
market	mercado
petrol station	posto de gasolina
police station	posto de policia
post office	correios
supermarket	supermercado
swimming pool	piscina
telephone	telefone
tourist information	poste de turismo
toilet (men/women)	quarto de banho (senhores/senhoras)

liners are in harbour and what is on at the local cinemas and theatre.

Supplementing this is the monthly *Madeira Island Bulletin*, free from hotels and the tourist office, which contains lots of useful information on restaurants, shops and entertainment.

On the radio you can pick up the BBC World Service and listen to hourly news reports. Madeira Tourist Radio 96mHZ FM (in English) broadcasts every day, except Sunday, at 5.45pm. The main theme of the show is restaurant recommendations; keep in mind that it is a commercial station where businesses pay for advertisements.

Most hotels in Funchal have satellite facilities so you can usually pick up 20 or so channels, including the American CNN channel, for news.

A wide range of English newspapers and magazines can be bought in hotel shops or city centre newsagents, usually the day after publication.

Money Matters

The money used on Madeira is the euro, which is divided into 100 cents. There are seven denominations of the Euro note: €5, €10, €20, €50, €100, €200 and €500; eight denominations of coins: 1 cent, 2 cents, 5 cents, 10 cents, 20 cents, 50 cents and €1 and €2.

Banks and Currency Exchange

All banks in Funchal offer currency exchange services and their rates are better than those of exchange bureaux or hotels. Banks are open Monday to Friday 8.30am–3pm, Saturday 9am–1pm, and several of the larger banks, located near the Sé (Cathedral) in

Avenida Arriaga, have hole-in-the-wall automatic exchange machines which operate 24 hours a day.

Exchange bureaux are open 9am–1pm and 2–7pm Monday to Friday, and 9am–1pm on Saturday. Whether you use a bank or a bureau, you have to present your passport when changing money, even for cash transactions. It pays to exchange as much as possible at one go, since there is a standard tax per transaction, no matter how large or small.

Cheques and Credit Cards
Traveller's cheques, Eurocheques and all the major credit cards can be used for obtaining money. Traveller's cheques and Eurocheques may also be used for paying bills in the more upmarket, tourist-oriented hotels, shops and restaurants, but credit cards are not yet accepted at all places.

For small-value transactions and in inexpensive local restaurants, cash is king. Surprisingly, even some hotels and restaurants with pretensions to status have yet to join the credit card age.

Value Added Tax
Value added tax is levied on most luxury goods at rates in excess of 12 per cent. So long as you come from a country outside the EU, you can claim a refund of this tax on large purchases in shops that participate in the Tax Free Shopping scheme; if so, they will have all the necessary forms and will explain how to obtain the refund.

National Holidays
1 January New Year's Day
February Shrove Tuesday

The day's headlines

March–April Good Friday
25 April Revolution Day
1 May Labour Day
April/May Corpus Christi
10 June Camões' Day
1 July Discovery of Madeira Day
15 August Assumption
21 August General Holiday
5 October Republic Day
1 November All Saints' Day, Independence
1 December Restoration Day
8 December Feast of the Immaculate Conception
25 December Christmas Day

Opening Hours
Banks Monday to Friday 8.30am–3pm.
Church 8am–1pm and 4–7pm but these can be subject to local variation.
Exchange bureaux (*cambios*) are open Monday to Friday 9am–1pm and 2–7pm; Saturdays 9am–1pm.

Shops Monday to Friday 9am–1pm and 3–7pm; Saturday 9am–1pm. These hours are observed strictly by most shops in central Funchal but the supermarket chains such as Lido Sol and Nova Esperanza are open 10am–9pm/10pm, seven days a week.

Pharmacies

In Portuguese a chemist or pharmacy is called a *farmácia.* They display a sign consisting of a white cross on a green background and are open Monday to Friday 9am–1pm and 3–7pm; Saturday 9am–1pm. All pharmacies have a notice showing which is on 24-hour duty.

The centrally situated Botica Inglesa, *Rua Câmara Pesteria 23–25* (*tel: (291) 220158*) caters to English-speaking visitors. There is also a pharmacy on call service (*tel: 118*).

Places of Worship

The Madeirans are Roman Catholic and mass is held regularly in churches all around the island. Madeira has its own Anglican chaplain and services are held at the Church of the Holy Trinity (better known as the English Church – *see p38*), *Rua do Quebra Costas 18* (*tel: (291) 220674*), at 11am every Sunday, and refreshments are served afterwards in the well-tended church gardens. The times of other services are posted in hotels and at the Tourist Information Centre, *Avenida Arriaga 18.*

Baptist services are held in English on Sundays at 11am at *Alto da Peno 126, Rua Silvestre, Quintino Frectas.* Catholic Mass is said in English at the Igreja da Penha, on Rua do Carvalho Araujo at 10.30am on Sundays.

Police

The fact that the police keep a low profile on Madeira is a tribute to the law-abiding nature of most Madeirans, but the police are there when you need them. Dial *112* in an emergency, otherwise *222022.* You can approach police officers for information or assistance: those wearing a red armband are there to help visitors; they speak another language as well as Portuguese – in most cases this means English.

Postal Services

Funchal's main post office (*correios*) is centrally located just up from the statue of Zarco on Avenida Zarco. Most of the staff here speak English. As well as postal transactions, you can also make overseas telephone calls from here, using special booths which enable you to pay once your call is finished.

The post office is open Monday to Friday 9am–1pm and 3–7pm, Saturday 9am–1pm, while the telephone booths stay open until 10pm. In the hotel district, there is also a post office in the Lido Sol supermarket complex, *Estrada Monumental 318*, which is open Monday to Friday 9am–7pm.

Public Transport
Taxis

Madeira's yellow cabs are an easy, cheap way of getting about Funchal. There are ranks at central points in the Hotel Zone and in the city centre, and you can hail any cab displaying a *livre* (free) sign. Hotels and restaurants will call a cab for you or you can phone for one yourself: **Funchal** *Tel: (291) 222000/222500.* **Machico** *Tel: (291) 2220911.*

Taxi journeys are metered within Funchal. There are set rates for longer journeys to specific destinations around the island. The official price list should be available for consultation in the taxi; copies are also displayed in the Tourist Information Centre, *Avenida Arriaga 18*, and on many hotel notice boards.

In theory the rates are also fixed for hiring a cab for the day or half-day, but in practice you can usually bargain the price down substantially. Hiring a taxi by the day means that you can work out your own tour itinerary, and if three or four people travel together this is cheaper than renting a self-drive car or joining an organised coach tour. Ask your hotel concierge, tour representative or a travel agent to recommend a driver who speaks English, knows the island well and drives safely. Otherwise, ring Central Taxis (*tel: (291) 230016*). Try to book taxi tours a day or two in advance, good drivers are in demand.

Most taxi drivers are honest (but *see p23*); if you feel you have been treated badly you should record the driver's number (displayed on the dashboard and painted on the outside of the front doors); reporting him to the police is a serious matter – simply to threaten to report the driver is probably sufficient to ensure a change of attitude.

Do not, under any circumstances, use unlicensed cabs whose smooth-talking drivers are out to rip you off, either through extortionate fares or by acting as touts for specific shops, restaurants, timeshare developments or other attractions.

Buses

If you intend to use buses (*autocarros*), be sure you have a lot of time and do not mind close contact with the local people, since they can get crowded. Orange town buses offer a very cheap way of getting around Funchal. The Tourist Office (*see pp186–7*) has a leaflet giving times and routes. The destination is indicated at the front of the bus. You can pay when you board but it is cheaper to buy tickets in advance in bulk from bus company kiosks on Avenida do Mar – the best deal is a seven-day pass available to visitors only, so you must produce your passport when you buy the ticket.

Long-distance buses are a useful form of transport for anyone who wants to explore Madeira's *levada* footpaths, since the bus system reaches most parts of the island far more cheaply than taxis. The problem is that the system is very confusing to the ordinary visitor.

You will find full details of routes and timetables in the daily English supplements to the *Notícias da Madeira* newspaper (distributed free to many hotels), but you will need the following information to work out which bus goes from where:

SAM buses (cream and green) (*Tel: (291) 229144*) operating routes 20, 23, 53, 60, 78, 113 and 156 depart from Rua Calouste Gulbenkian and service the east and northeast of the island, including the airport.

Rodoeste buses (red, grey and white) (*Tel: (291) 220148*), operating routes 1, 4, 6, 7, 96, 107, 139, 148 and 154, leave from the Rua Ribeira Joao Gomes in Funchal.

Three companies operate routes 2, 29, 77, 103, 136 and 155. Ask your hotel concierge, or enquire at the Tourist Information Centre, *Avenida Arriaga 18*, for the latest information on these bus routes and companies.

Senior Citizens

Senior citizens' concessions in Madeira are available only to Portuguese nationals. Several UK-based tour operators specialising in Madeira offer extremely cheap rates on winter-break holidays of three weeks or more. Given Madeira's mild winter climate and low cost of living, this can be a very attractive alternative to spending winter in chilly northern Europe.

Sustainable tourism

Thomas Cook is a strong advocate of ethical and fairly traded tourism and believes that the travel experience should be as good for the places visited as it is for the people who visit them. That's why we firmly support The Travel Foundation: a charity that develops solutions to help improve and protect holiday destinations, their environment, traditions and culture. To find out what you can do to make a positive difference to the places you travel to and the people who live there, please visit *www.thetravelfoundation.org.uk*

Student/Youth Travel

If you are visiting Madeira on a budget, go for lower-cost flights via Lisbon rather than the more expensive direct flights, travel by bus and shop for food in local markets. Cheap accommodation can be had in *pensãos* (pensions) in most villages, though Funchal is geared to the upmarket traveller and has little in the way of budget accommodation.

Some visitors to Madeira dispense with typical accommodations preferring to camp (*see* Camping, *p175*) at one of the

Country bus stop

two designated campsites on the island. Bear in mind that although sleeping under the stars might be peaceful and beautiful, it is illegal on Madeira and you could face expensive fines.

Telephones

Local calls are easily made from coin-operated phones which take 20 and 50 cents and euro coins. For international calls, it is cheapest to buy a card from post offices and shops displaying the Credifone symbol and use the card phones to be found all over Funchal.

Alternatively, you can use the metered telephone booths at the main post office (*see* Postal Services, *p183*) and pay at the end of your call. You can, of course, dial direct from your hotel room, and pay a hefty premium for the convenience.

To call another European country dial *00* followed by the country code (Ireland *353*, UK *44*, then the area code, minus the initial *0*, then the subscriber number).

To call outside Europe, dial *171* followed by the country code:
USA and **Canada** *001*
Australia *0061*
New Zealand *0064*
South Africa *0027*
Directory Enquiries (Madeira) *118*
Operator *090*
International Operator *171*

Time

Madeira observes Greenwich Mean Time (GMT) in winter (end of September to end of March) and GMT plus 1 hour in summer. Thus in summer, Madeira is 5 hours ahead of Eastern Standard Time, 8 hours ahead of Pacific Time, 1 hour behind Lisbon and much of Europe, 2 hours behind South Africa, 9 behind Australia and 12 behind New Zealand.

Tipping

On Madeira, nobody demands tips as a right or treats you differently if you do not tip – indeed, people seem pleasantly surprised when a tip is offered to them. It is normal to tip 10–15 per cent in bars and restaurants. Many expensive restaurants also include a 10 per cent service charge on the bill.

Toilets

Hotels, bars, restaurants and museums have toilets for public use, and these are usually modern and clean.

Doors are usually marked *senhoras* (women) and *senhores* (men); fortunately for those who cannot remember which is which, they usually carry some kind of identifying symbol as well.

Tourist Information

Funchal's Tourist Information Office is centrally located at *Avenida Arriaga 18* and is open Monday to Friday 9am–8pm, Saturday 9am–6pm.

The English-speaking staff are genuinely helpful and will supply free maps as well as answers to just about any question you may have. You can telephone as well (*tel: (291) 211900*) but the office is really geared to the needs of people who visit in person.

Within the office there is also a currency exchange bureau and a booking desk where you can sign up for organised tours.

There are smaller offices, with more restricted openings, one in the arrivals lounge at Santa Catarina Airport and also in Machico, at Nossa Senhora do Amparo Fort (*tel: (291) 962289*).

Tourist Offices Overseas
For information on Madeira before you leave home, there are Portuguese National Tourist Offices in many cities around the world, including:
Canada 60 Bloor St West, Suite 1005, Toronto, Ontario M4W 3B8. *Tel: +1 416–921 7376.*
UK 22–25A Sackville St, London W1X 1DE. *Tel: (020) 7494 1441.*
USA 590 Fifth Avenue, 4th Floor, New York, NY 10036–4704. *Tel: +1(212) 3544403.*

Travel Agents
There are numerous travel agents in the Hotel Zone and in central Funchal and they will help you choose the coach excursions, boat trips, *levada* walking tours or jeep safaris that are best for you. The following are among the leading agents and operators:
Blandy's Everything from round-the-island tours to folk evenings or mini cruises (*Avenia Zarco 2. Tel: (291) 200620*).
Madeira Explorers Levada & Leisure Walks Trained guides lead multi- and single-day walking tours of Madeira's *levadas*, mountains and ridges (*Centro Comercial Monumental Lido, Shop 5, 3rd floor, Estrada Monumental. Tel: (291) 763701. www.madeira-levada-walks.com*)
Strawberry World This is one-stop shopping for things to see and do on Madeira; from car hire, bus tours, walks and mountain climbing to restaurants and accommodation. The company

offers many types of holiday packages (*Centro Comercial Monumental Lido, 3rd floor, office 2 Estrada Monumental. Tel: (291) 762421. www.strawberry-world.com*)
Terras de Adventura Tourismo (Trails of Adventure) This company is definitely for the thrill seekers no matter what age; choose from sea kayaking, diving, parasailing or mountain climbing. Biking, jeep safaris and four-wheel biking are just a few of the other things they offer that you can do on your own or with a guide/group (*Caminho do Amparo 25. Tel: (291) 266818 or 261018. www.madeira-island.com/aventura*)

The Thomas Cook Tour Operations Office The office is not staffed on a regular basis. If you have questions or an emergency it would be best to call their mobile and leave a message. *Rua Dom Carlos, Funchal. Mobile tel: 00351 (962) 404794.*

Travellers with Disabilities
Facilities for visitors with disabilities to Madeira are limited. TAP Air Portugal has provision for passengers with wheelchairs, and luxury hotels such as the Savoy and Madeira Palácio are able to offer accommodation of an acceptable standard, as can the Luamar Hotel on Porto Santo.

Inspired by the local colours

ACKNOWLEDGEMENTS

Thomas Cook Publishing wishes to thank the following photographers, libraries and associations for their assistance in the preparation of this book, and to whom the copyright in the photographs belongs.

SPECTRUM COLOUR LIBRARY 20, 21, 37, 78
NEIL SETCHFIELD 172a, 172b
PICTURES COLOUR LIBRARY 41, 131, 134, 135, 158
DIRECÇÃO REGIONAL TOURISMO DA MADEIRA 9, 12, 25, 39, 52, 53, 84 (Marcial Fernandes), 85, 86 (Antonio Spinola), 89, 125, 143, 149, 155, 168, 180

The remaining pictures are held in the AA PHOTO LIBRARY and were taken by: JON WYAND, with the exception of pages 8, 17, 19, 23, 24, 28, 30, 31, 46a, 47a, 80b, 81a, 101, 106, 116a, 130b, 139a, 152, 153a, 153b, 157, 164a, 164b which were taken by PETER BAKER, and page 154a taken by WYN VOYSEY.

Index: MARIE LORIMER

Proofreading: JOANNE OSBORN for CAMBRIDGE PUBLISHING MANAGEMENT LIMITED

Travellers **Madeira**

Feedback Form

Please help us improve future editions by taking part in our reader survey. Every returned form will be acknowledged. To show our appreciation we will send you a voucher entitling you to £1 off your next *Travellers* guide or any other Thomas Cook guidebook ordered direct from Thomas Cook Publishing. Just take a few minutes to complete and return this form to us.

We'd also be glad to hear of your comments, updates or recommendations on places we cover or you think that we ought to cover.

1. Which of the following tempted you into buying your *Travellers* guide?
   (Please tick as many as appropriate)

   a) the price   ☐

   b) the cover   ☐

   c) the content   ☐

   d) other _____

2. What do you think of:

   a) the cover design _____

   b) the design and layout styles within the book _____

   c) the content_____

   d) the maps _____

3. Please tell us about any features that in your opinion could be changed, improved or added in future editions of the book or any other comments you would like to make concerning this book _____

   _____

   _____

   _____

   _____

4. What is the single most useful/helpful aspect of this book?_____

   _____

cut along the dotted line

5. Have you purchased other *Travellers* guides in the series?

    a) yes   ☐

    b) no   ☐

    If yes, please specify which titles _____

6. Would you purchase other *Travellers* guides?

    a) yes   ☐

    b) no   ☐

    If no, please specify why not _____

Your age category: ☐ under 21   ☐ 21–30   ☐ 31–40   ☐ 41–50   ☐ 51+

Mr/Mrs/Miss/Ms/Other

Surname_____ Initials_____

Full address (please include postal or zip code):_____

_____

_____

Daytime telephone number: _____

Email address: _____

Please detach this page and send it to: The Series Editor, *Travellers* guides, Thomas Cook Publishing, PO Box 227, The Thomas Cook Business Park, Units 15–16, Coningsby Road, Peterborough PE3 8SB, United Kingdom.

Alternatively, you can email us at: *books@thomascook.com*